TOTES TWO

a coloradoodle coloring book

by

Patricia Burke

Cover Art Created by Patricia Burke

ISBN: 978-1-951576-18-9

Book title
a coloradoodle coloring book

Find Other
coloradoodle coloring books here:

https://www.amazon.com/author/patriciaburke.doodlist

Shoe-dles
Hearts
Petal Pusher
Shoe-dles 2
Simply Mandala
Petal Pusher 2
Another Really Big Ginormous Book of Doodles
Encircled
Heartfelt
Sunflowers
Totes
Coloring Christmas
Big Hearts
Petal Pusher 3
Mini Mandala
Ovalicious
Tubby Totes
Catitude
Patterns by Patty
Spring Fling
Kaleidoscopes
EGGED!
Totes Two

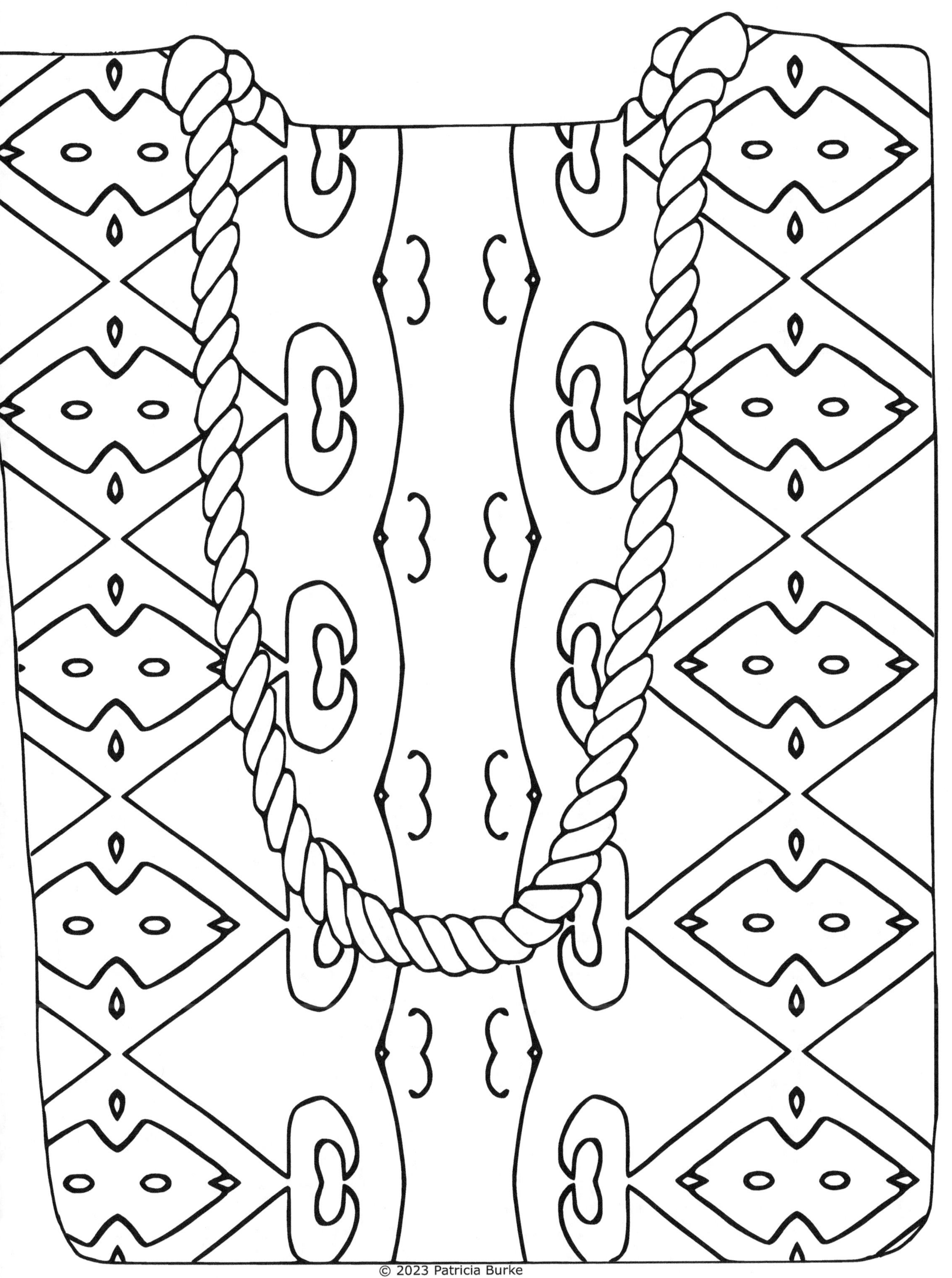

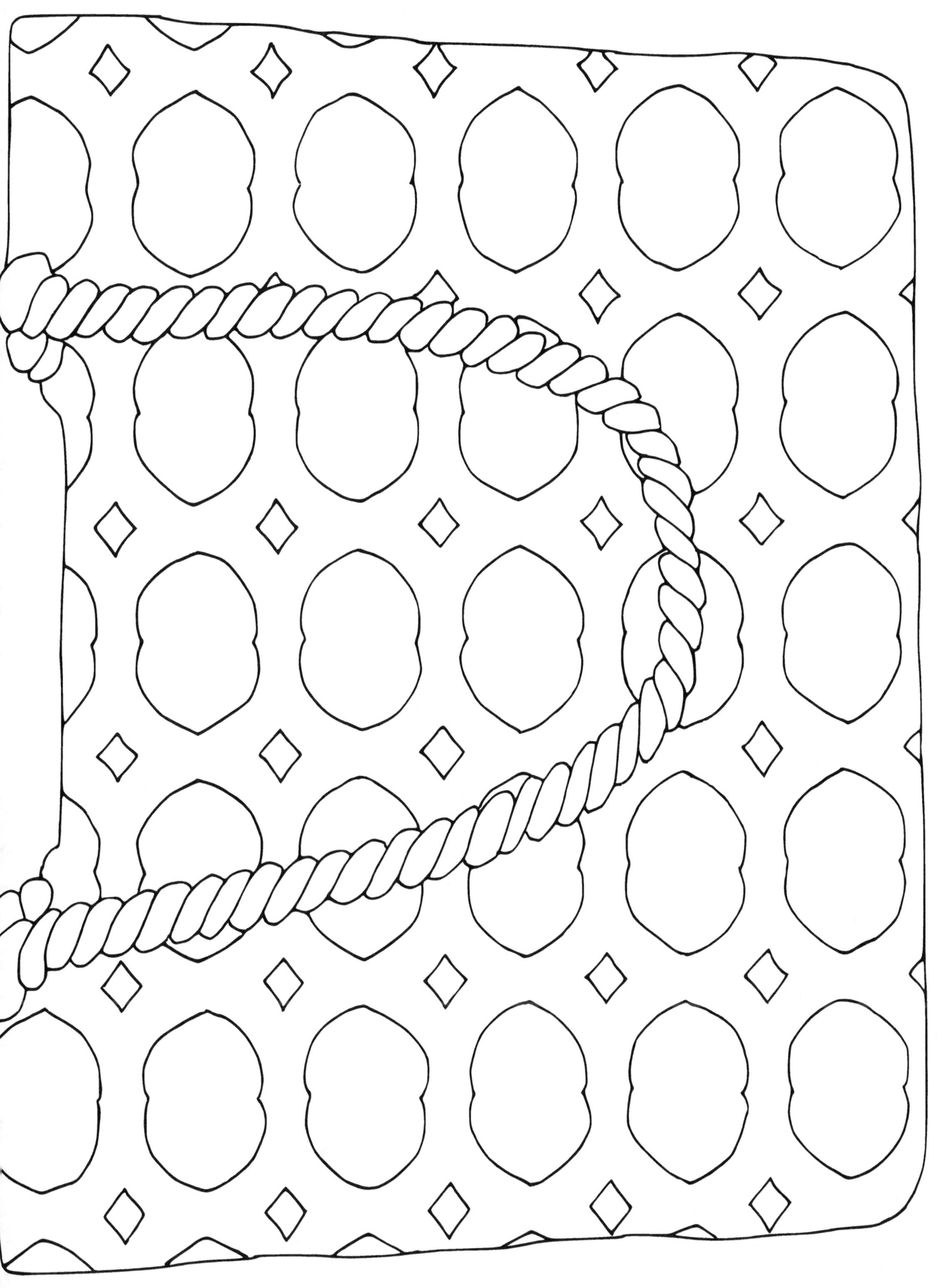

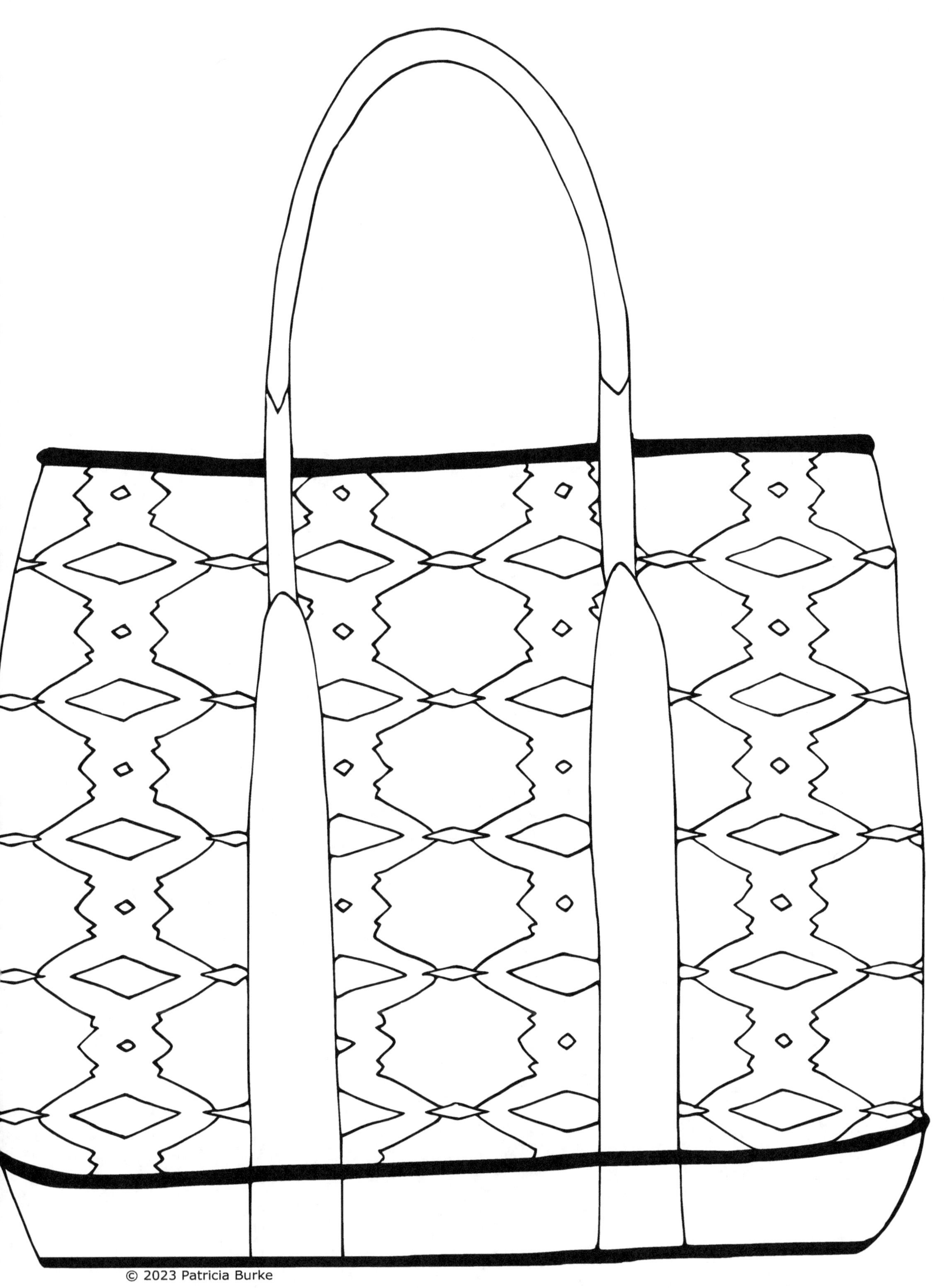

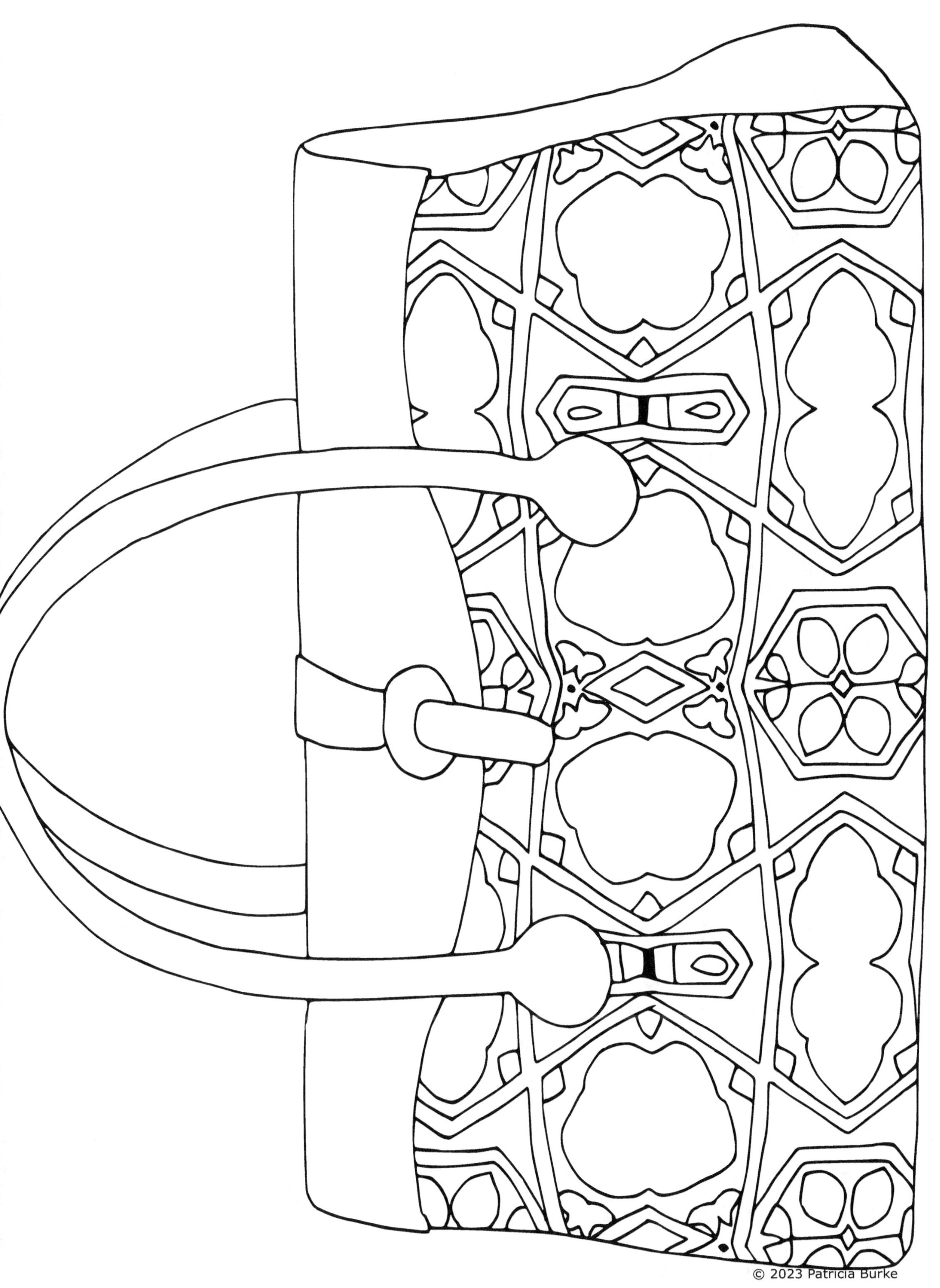

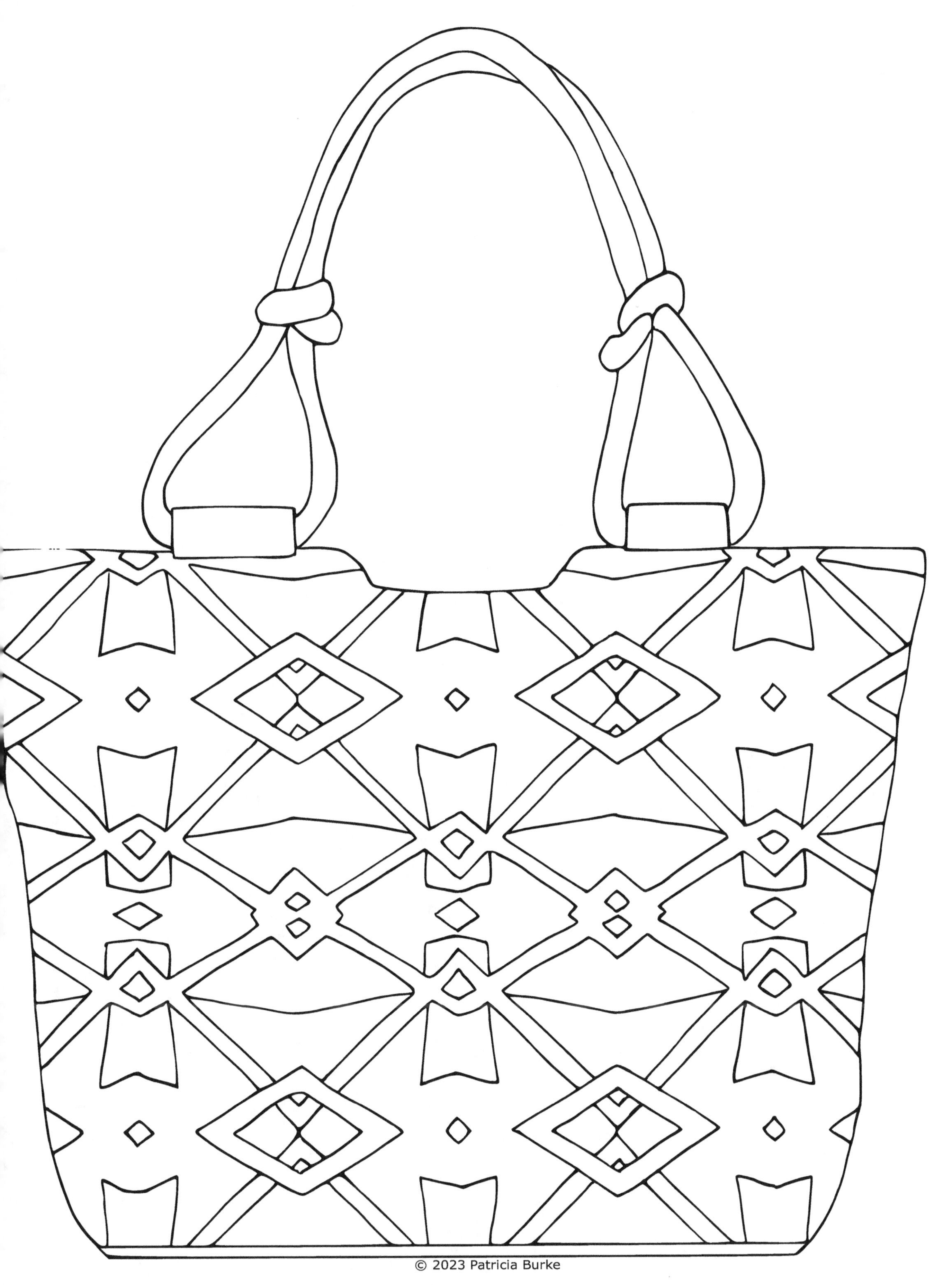

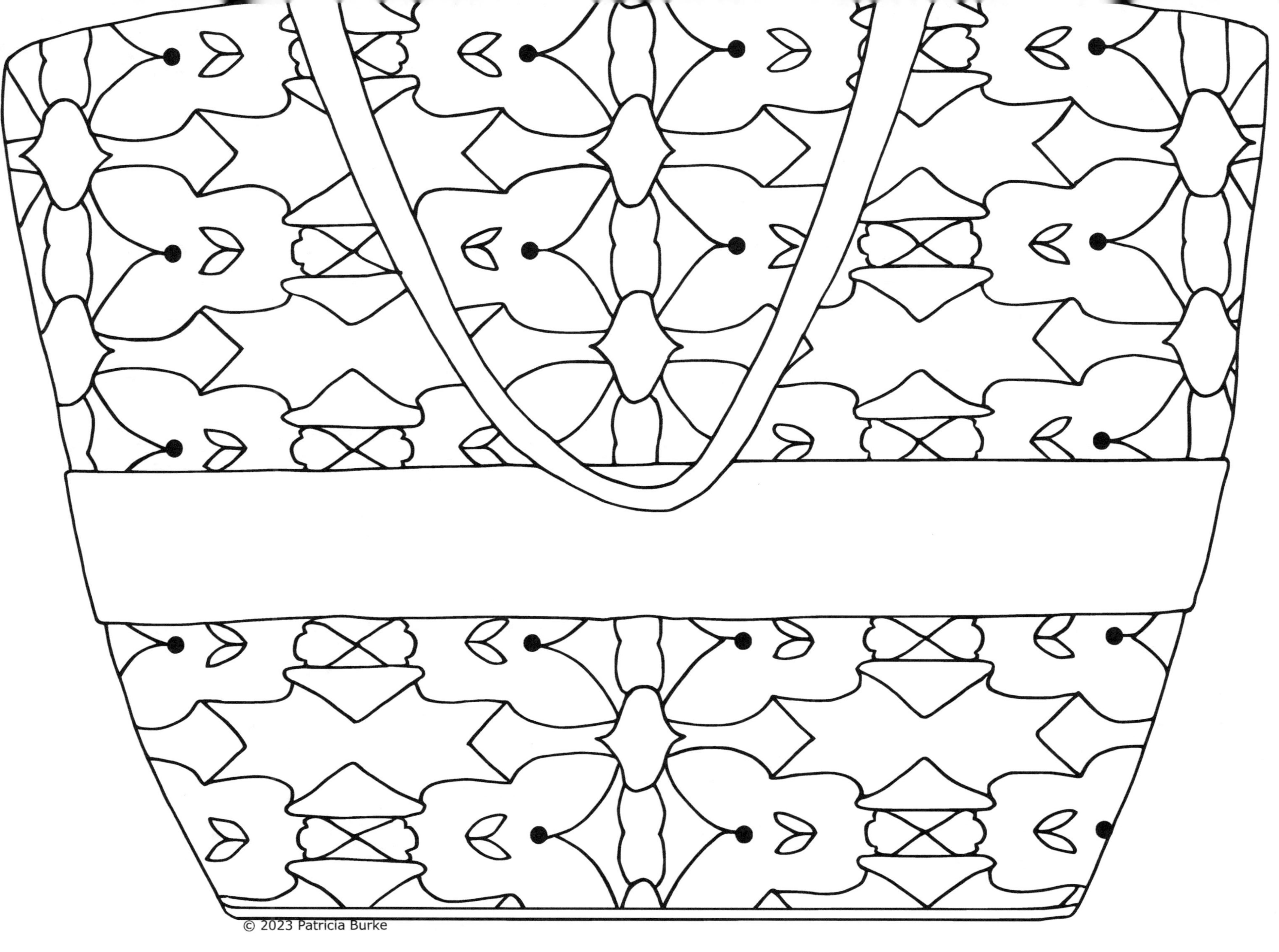

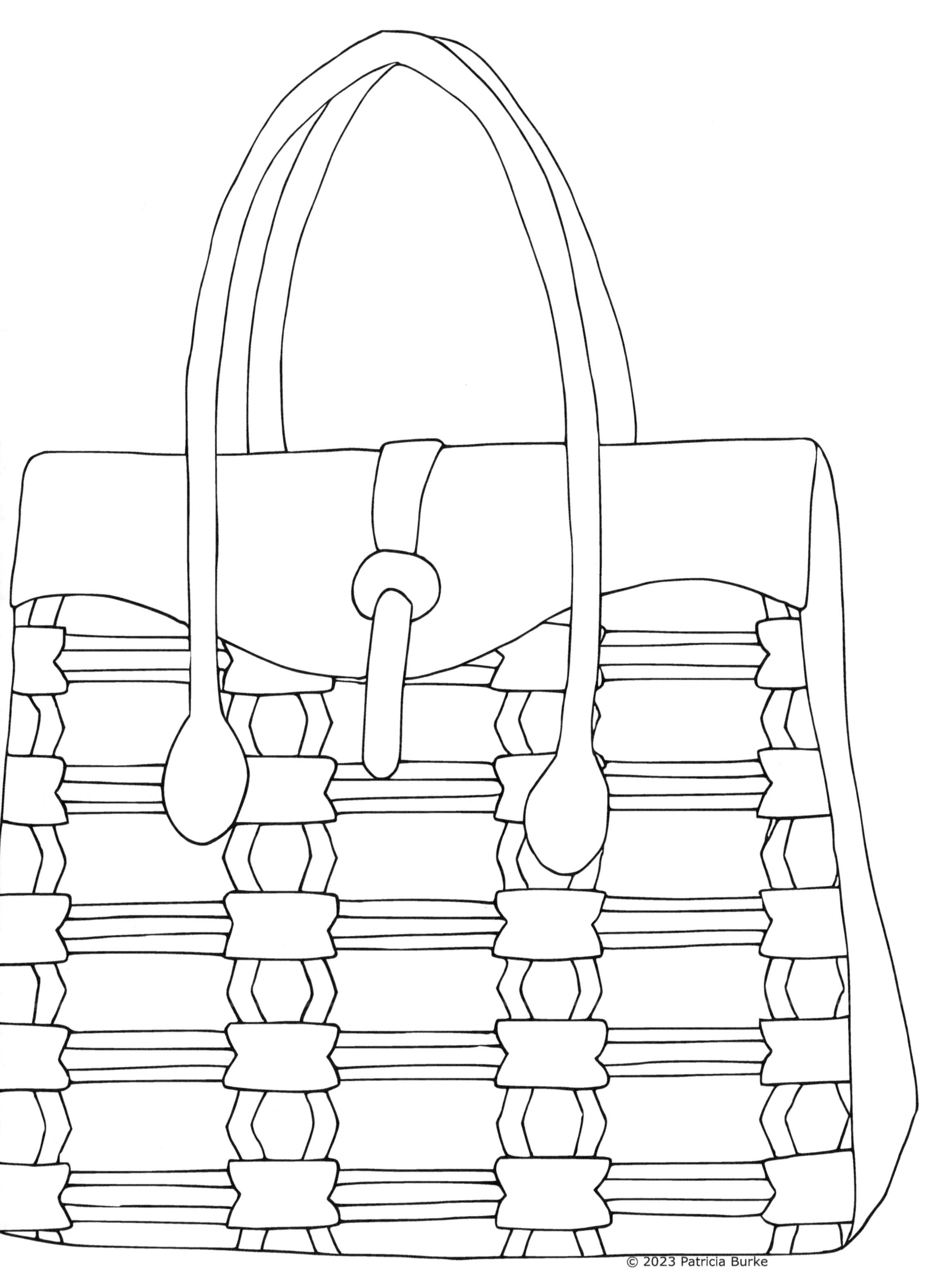

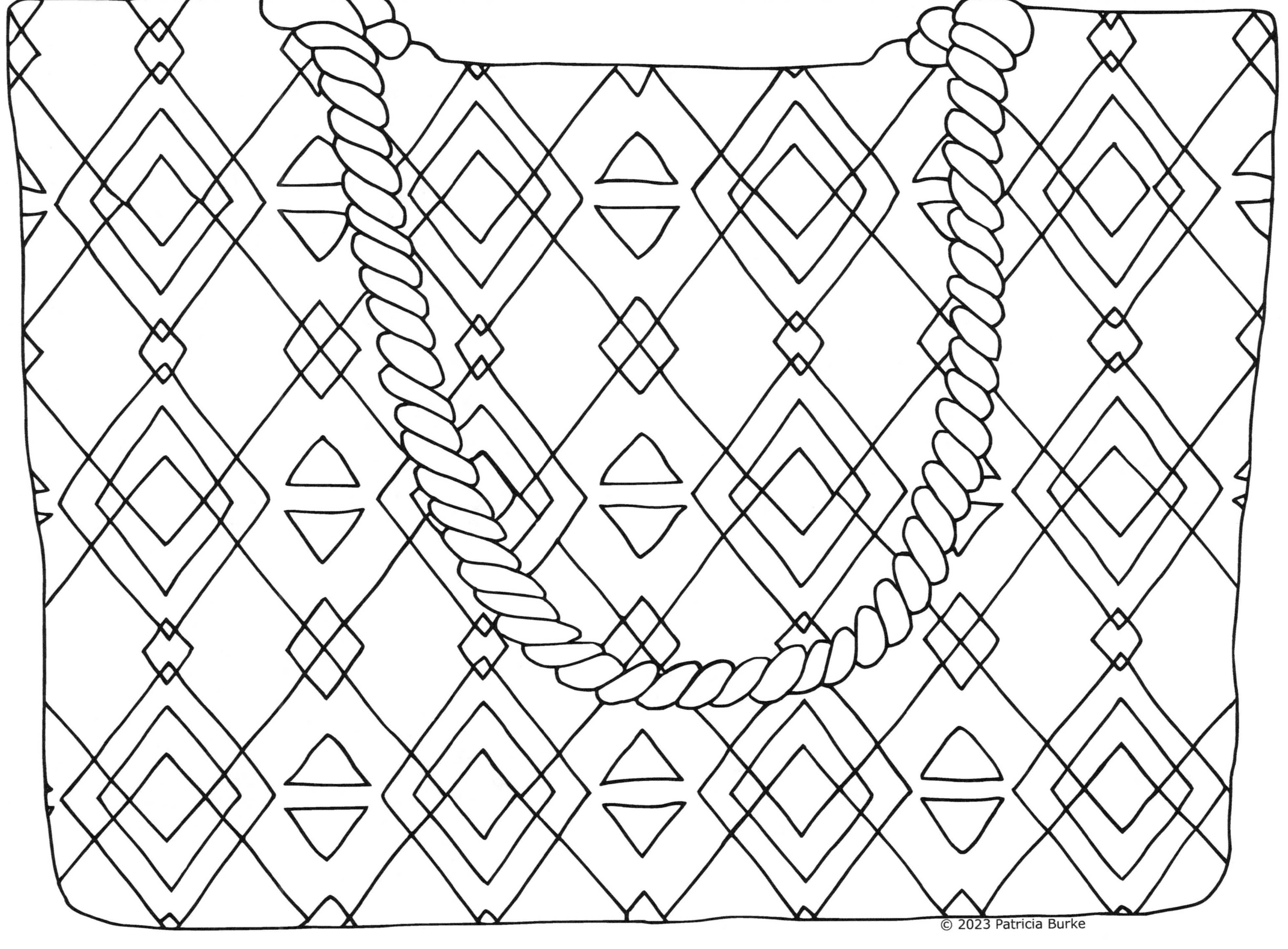

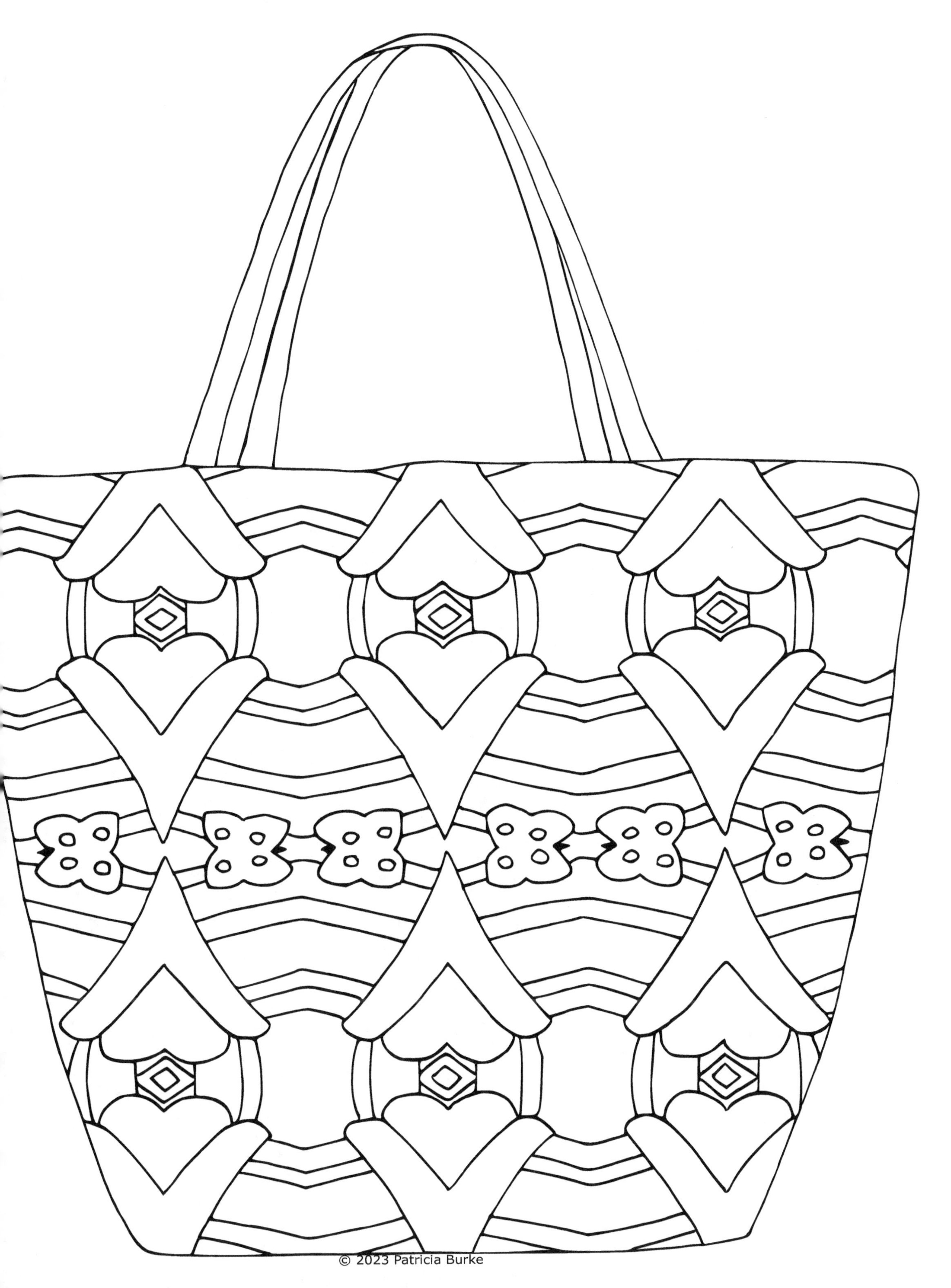

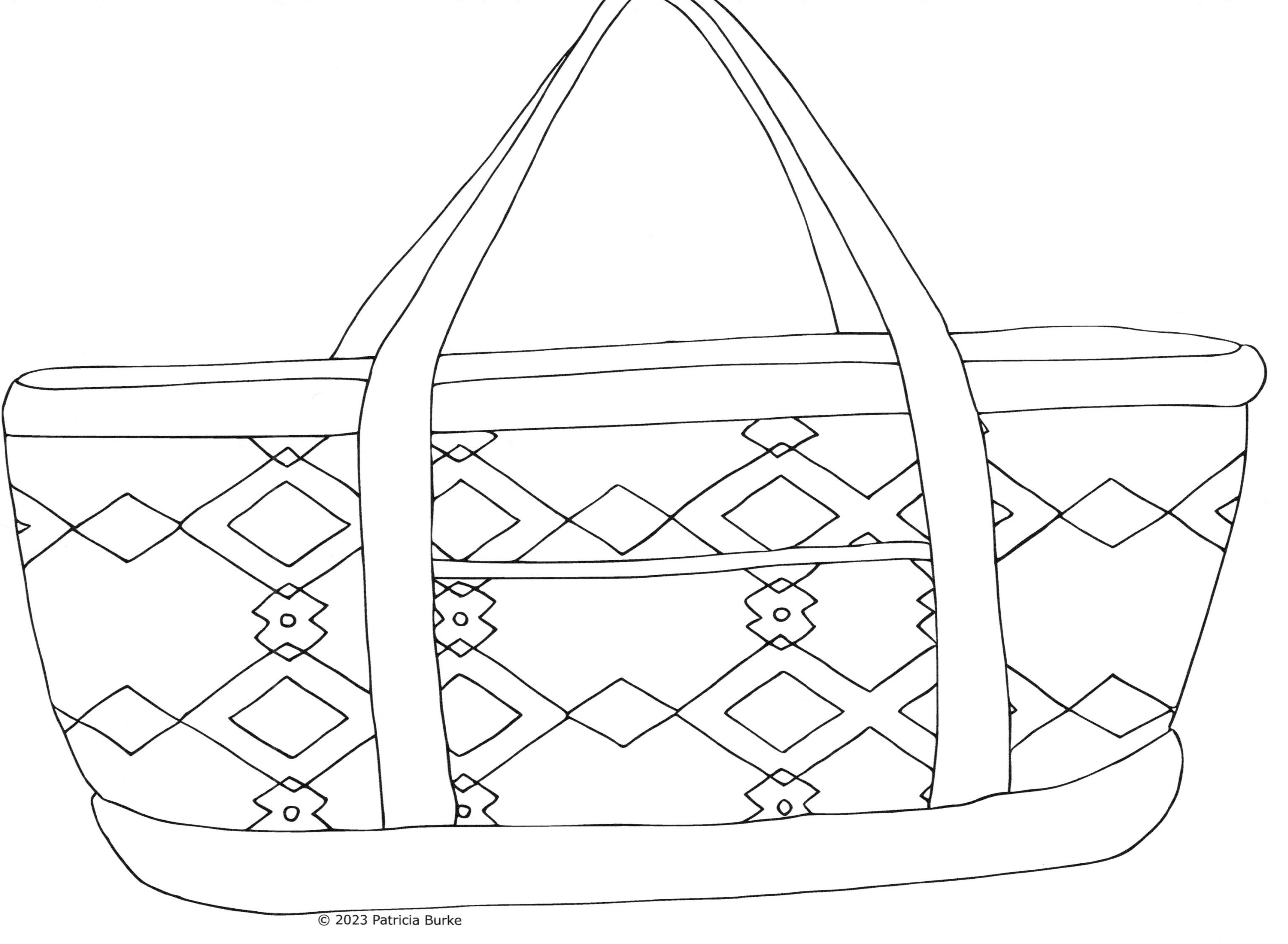

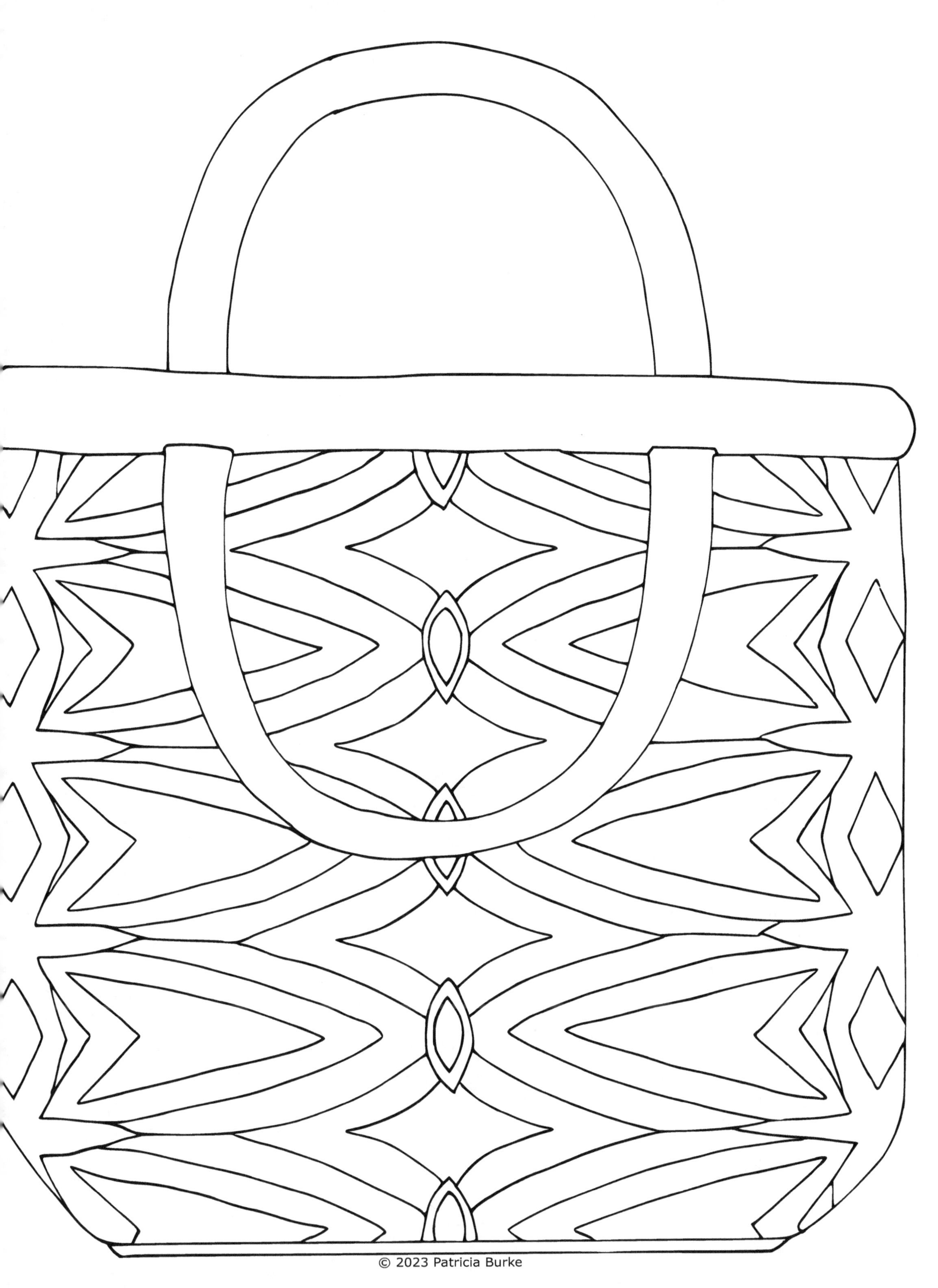

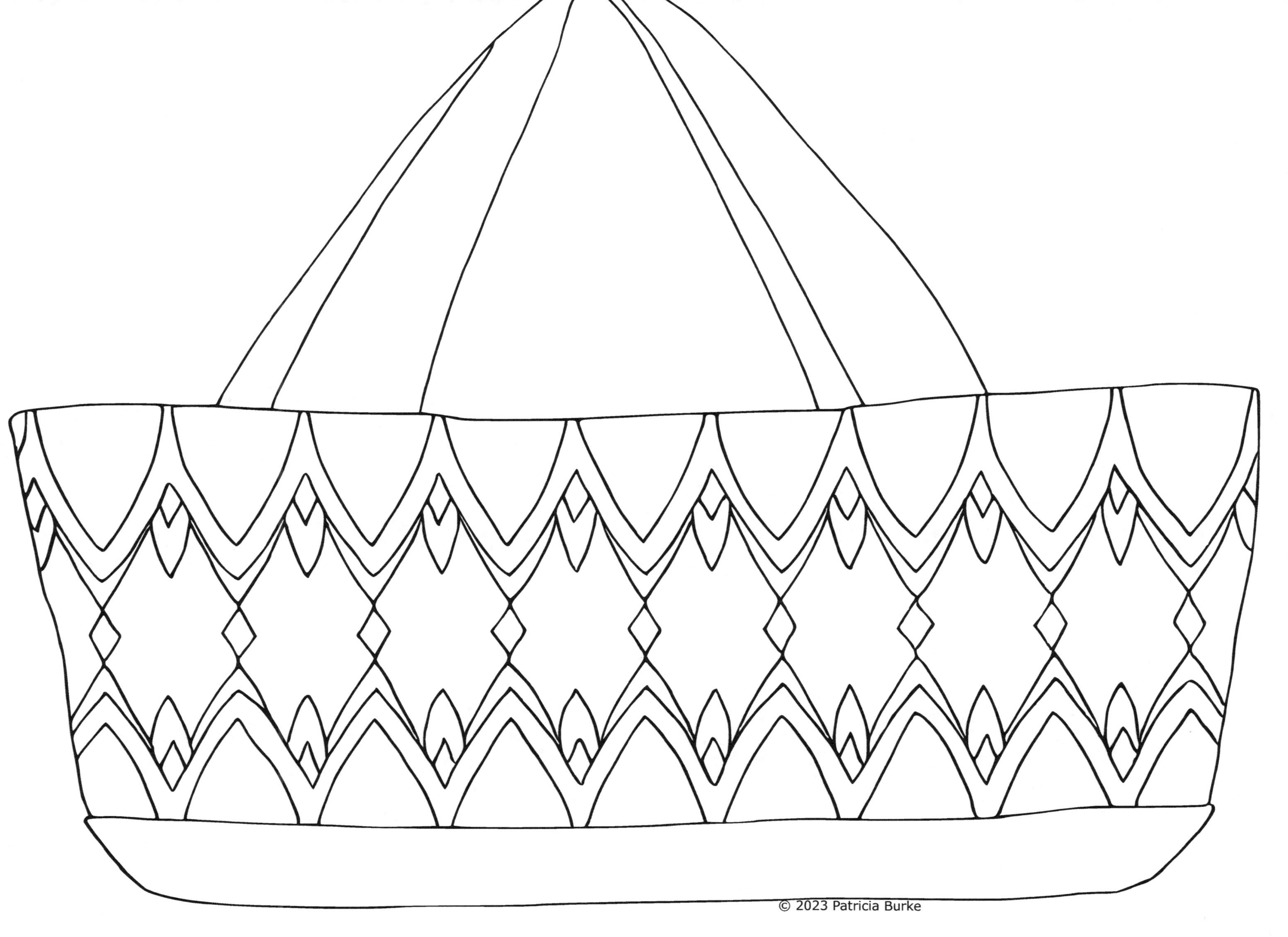

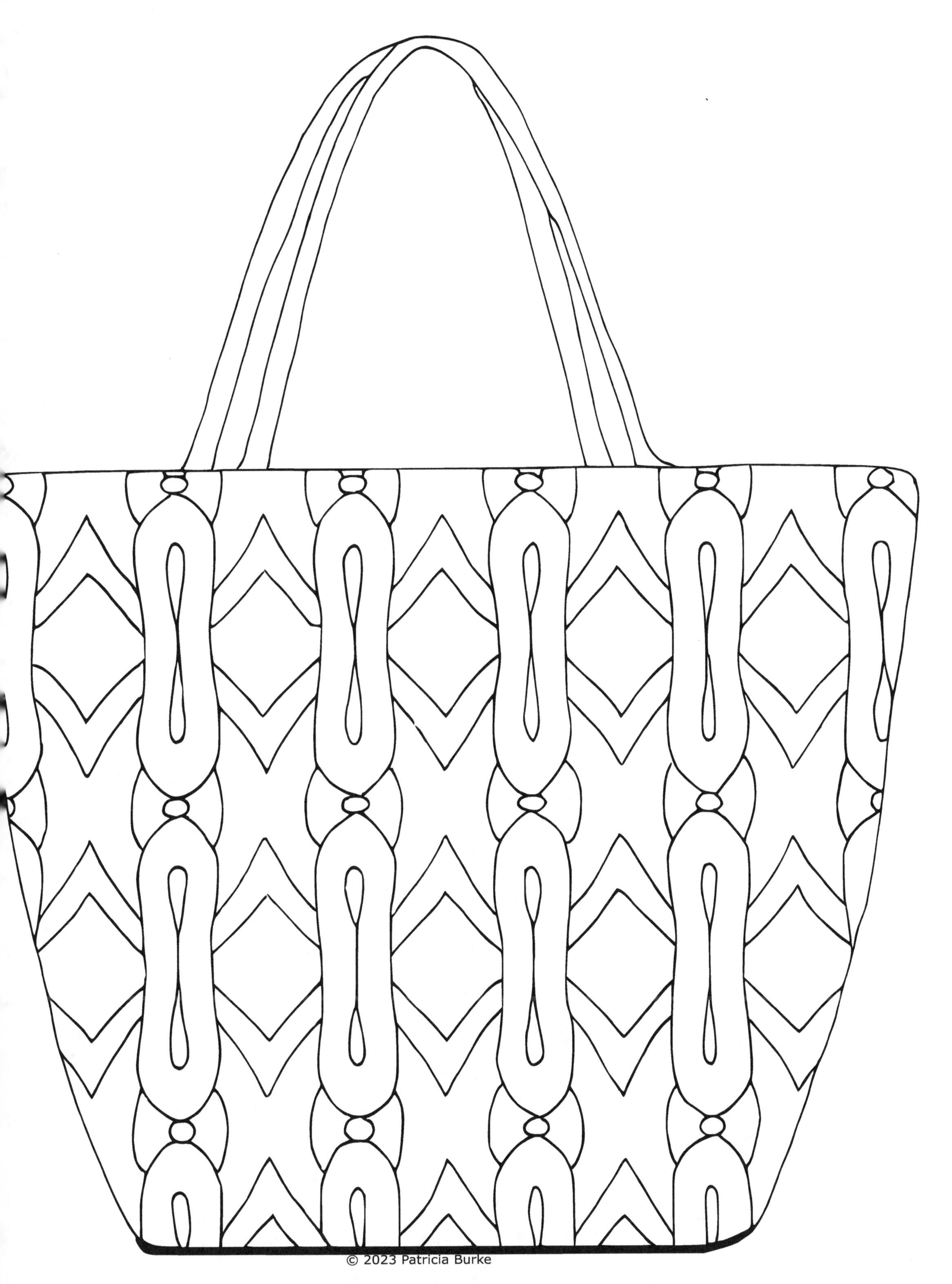

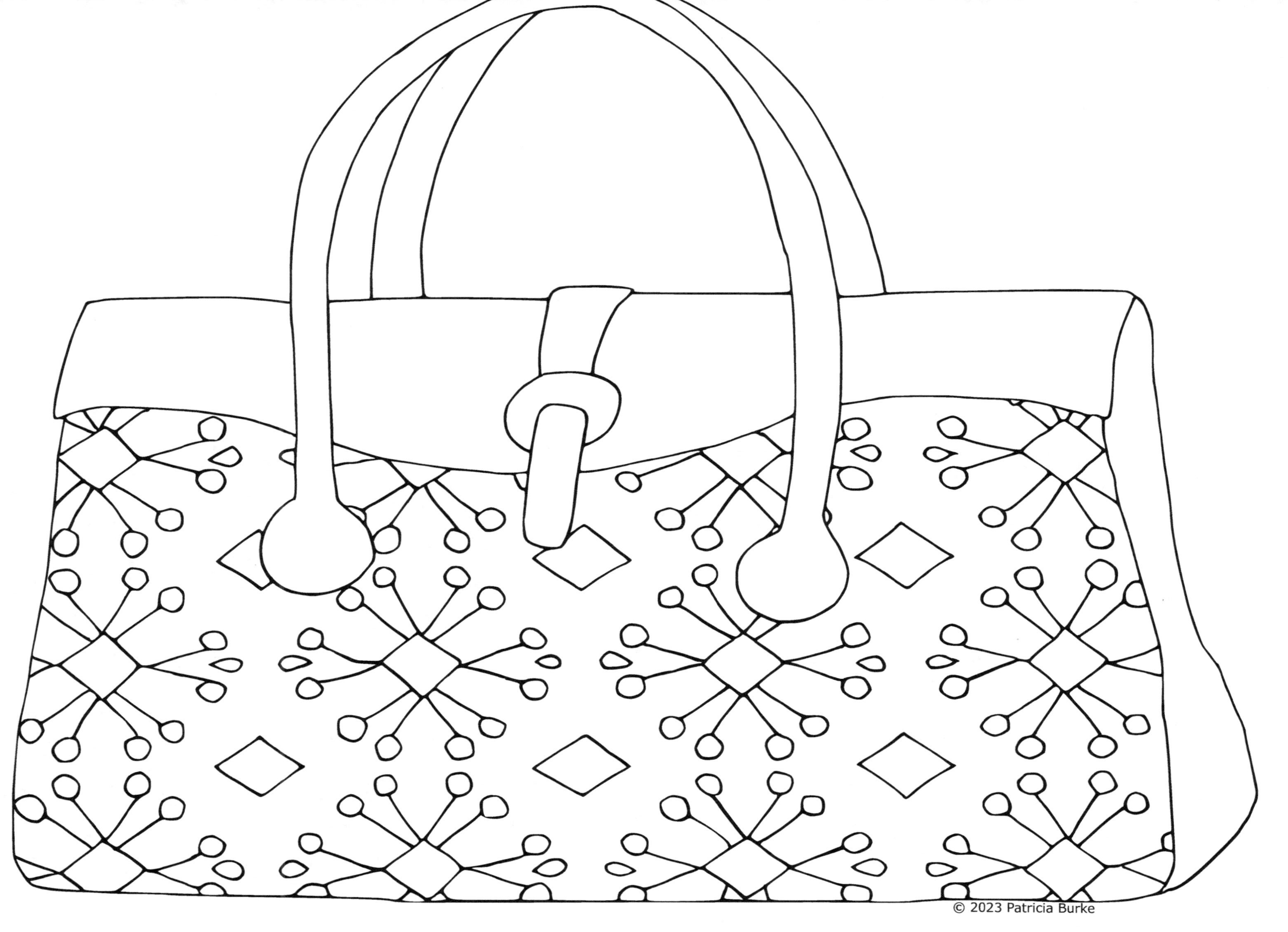

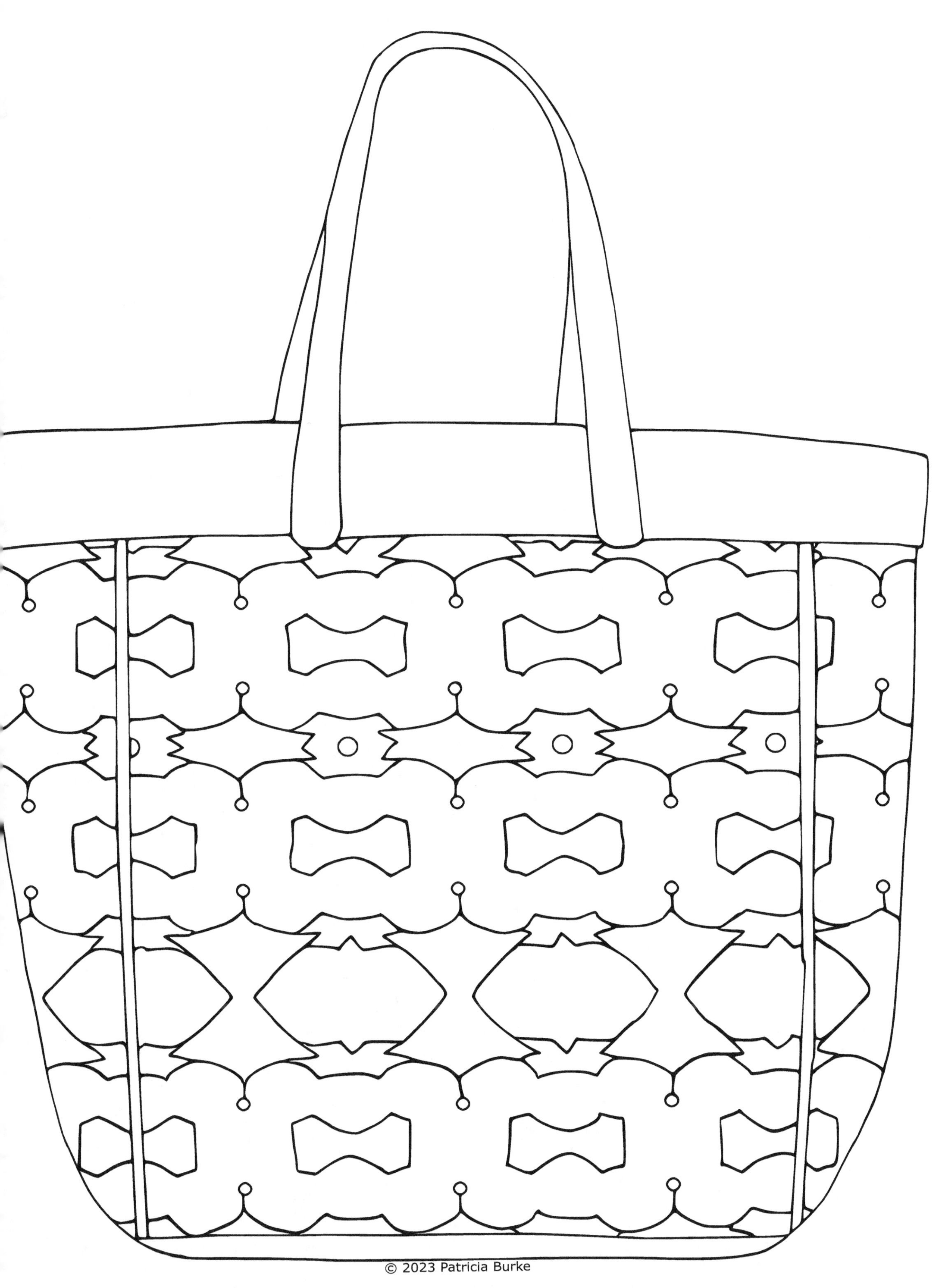

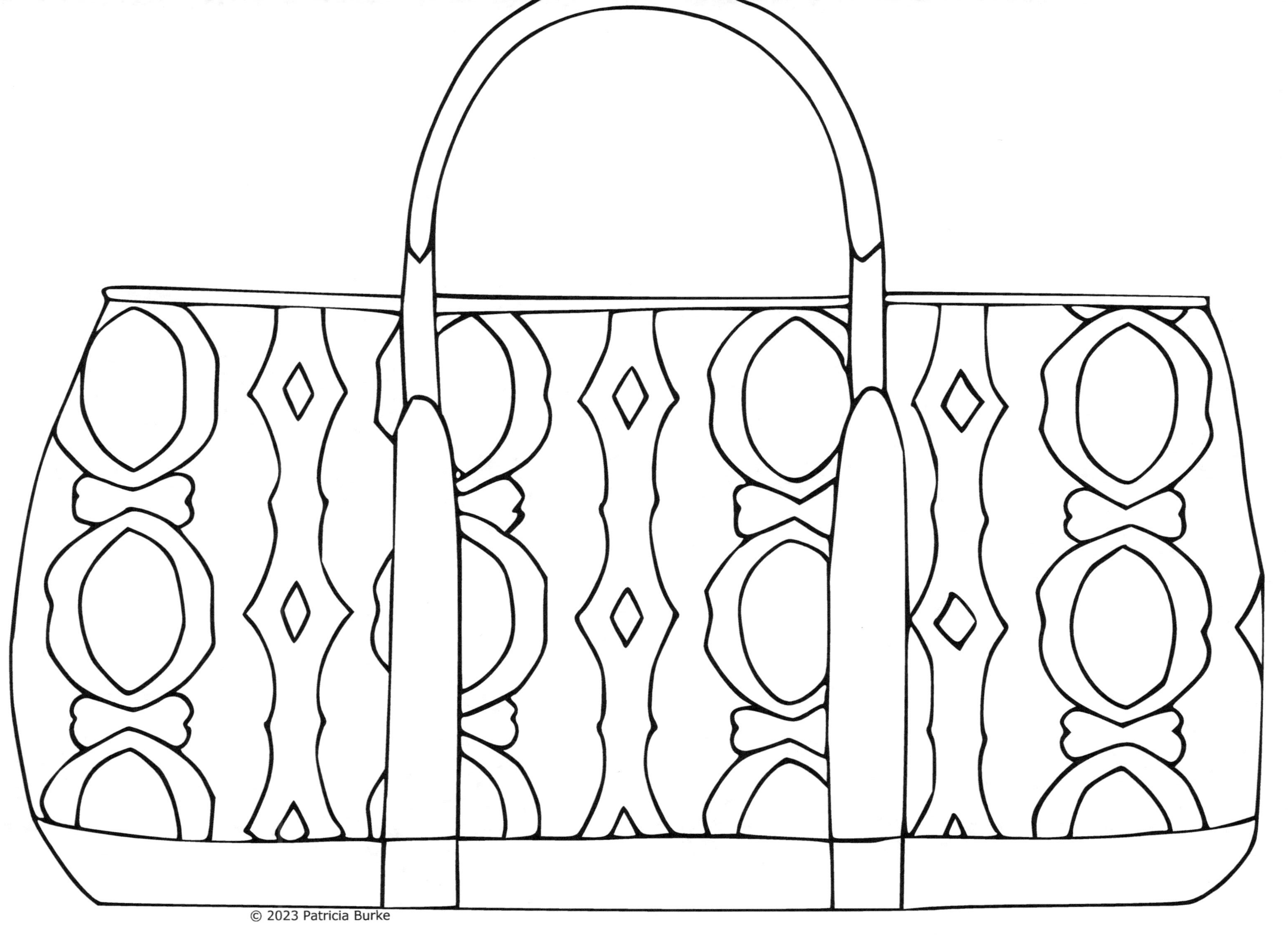

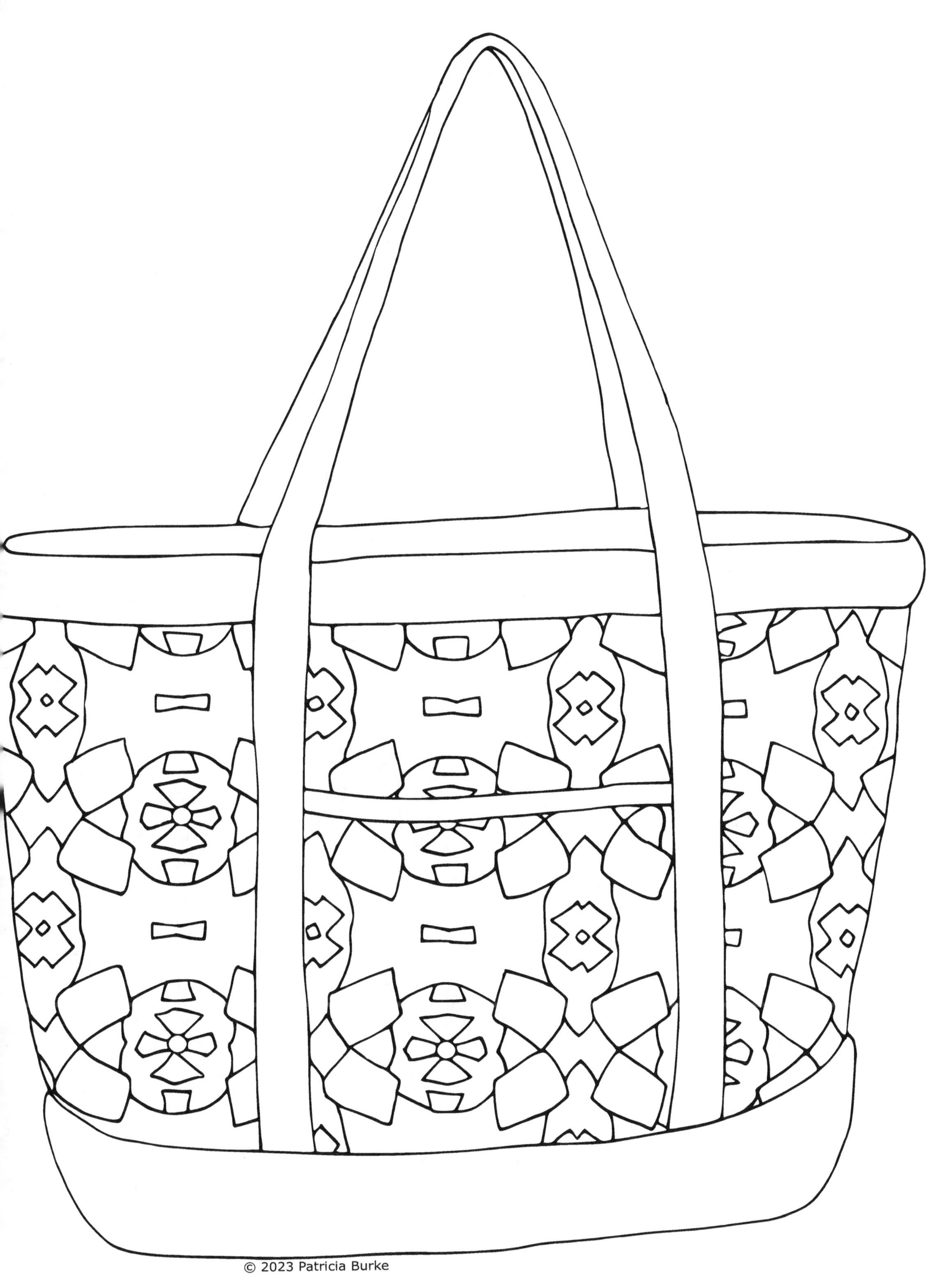

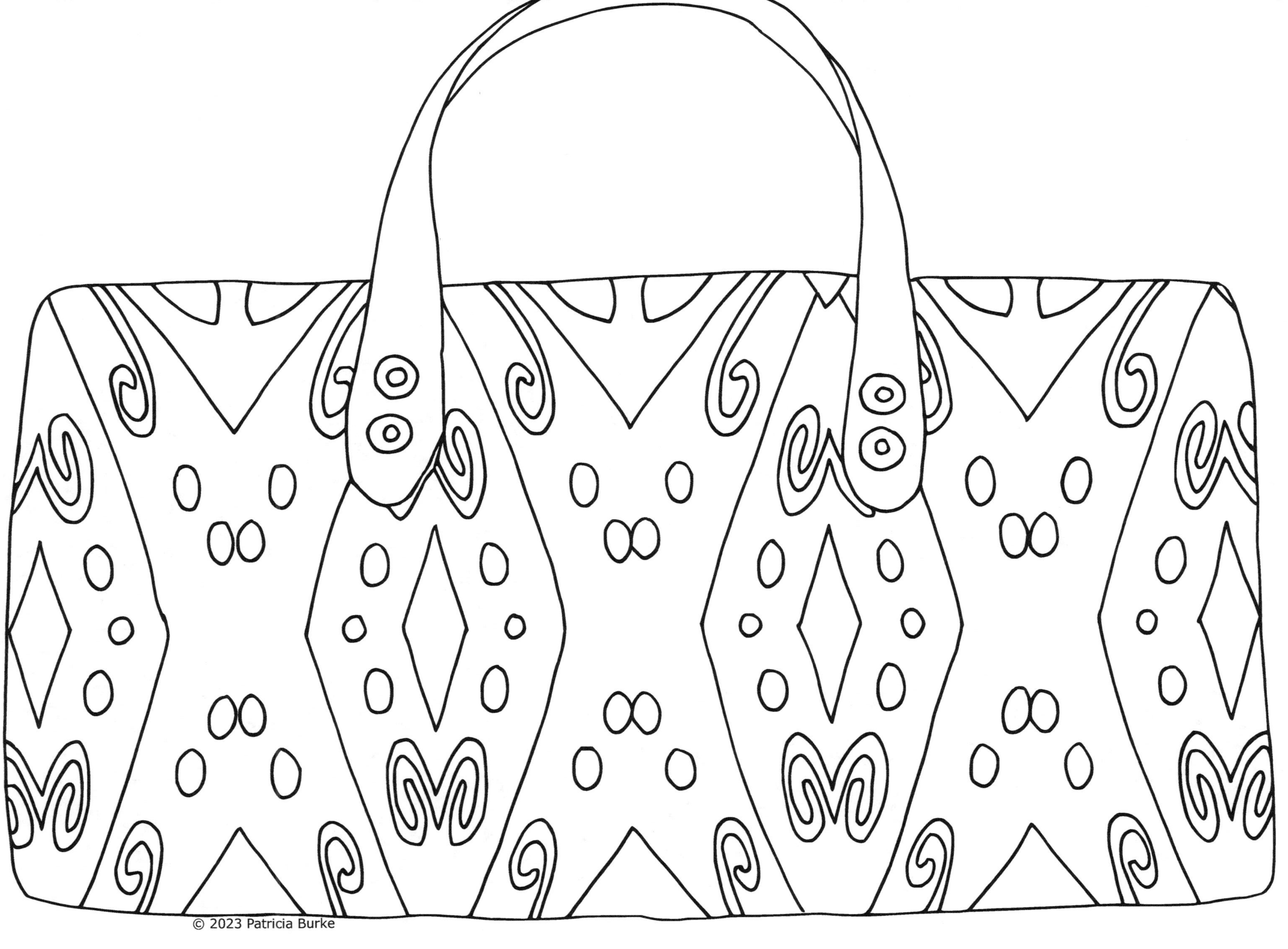

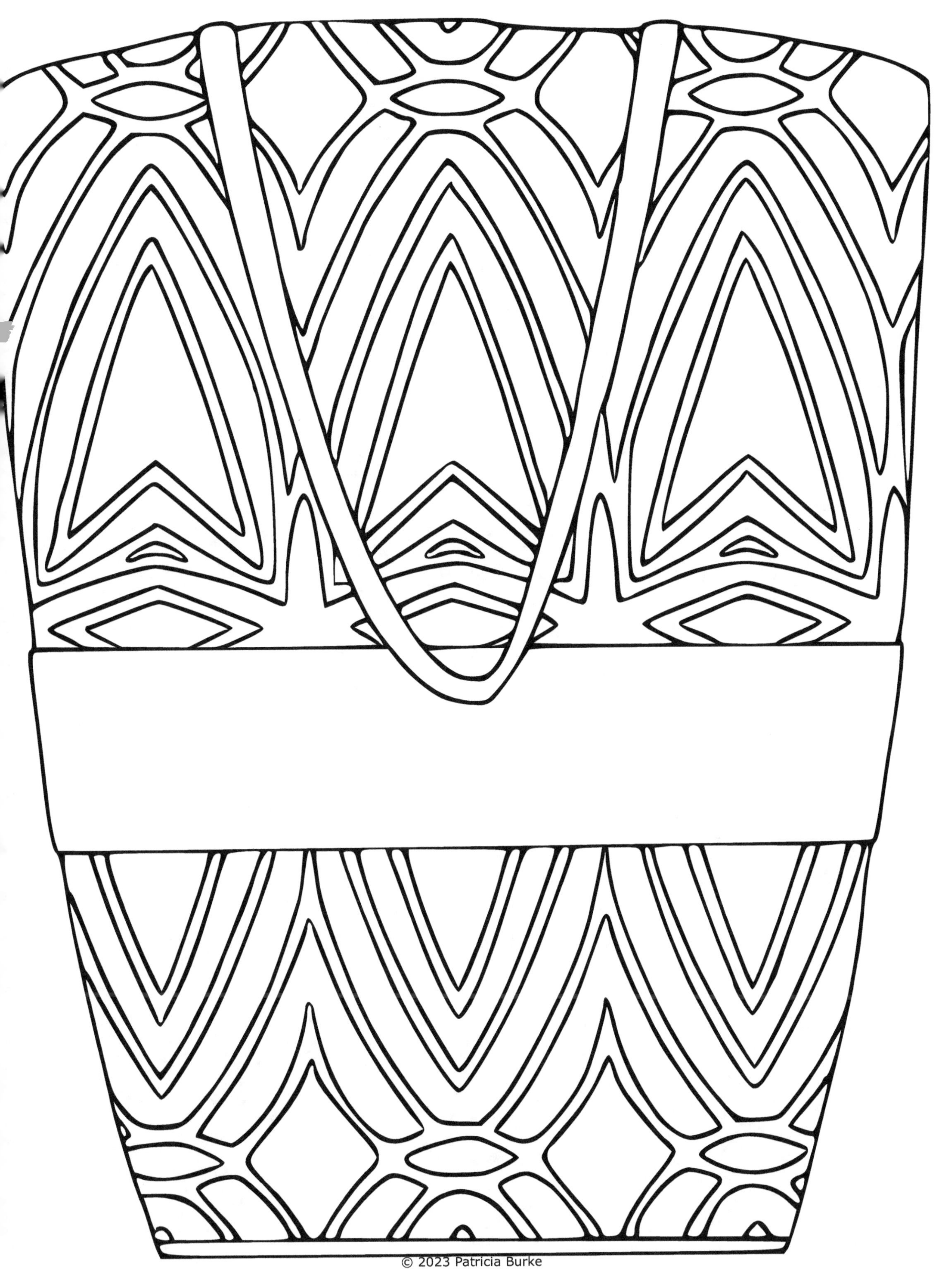

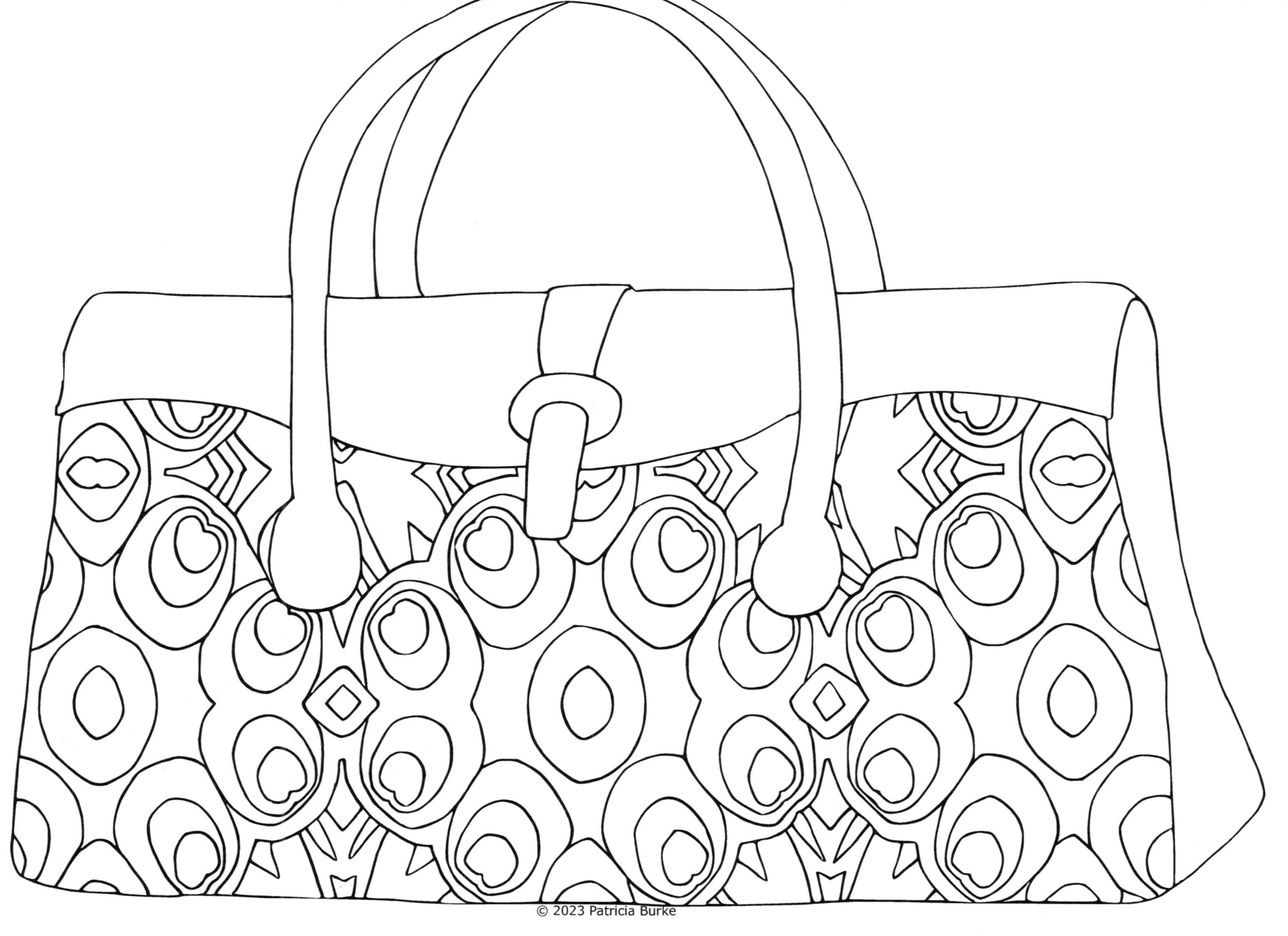

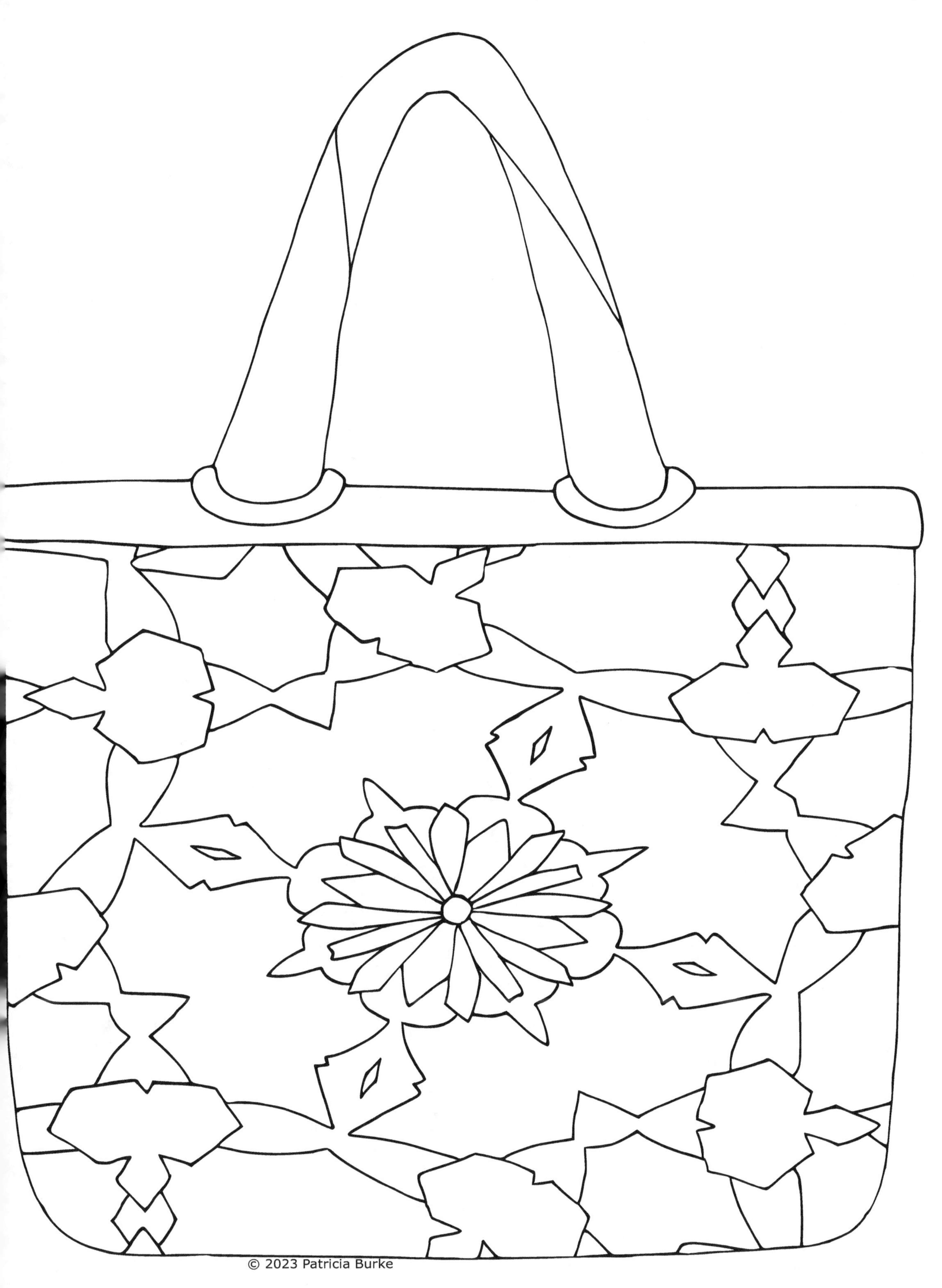

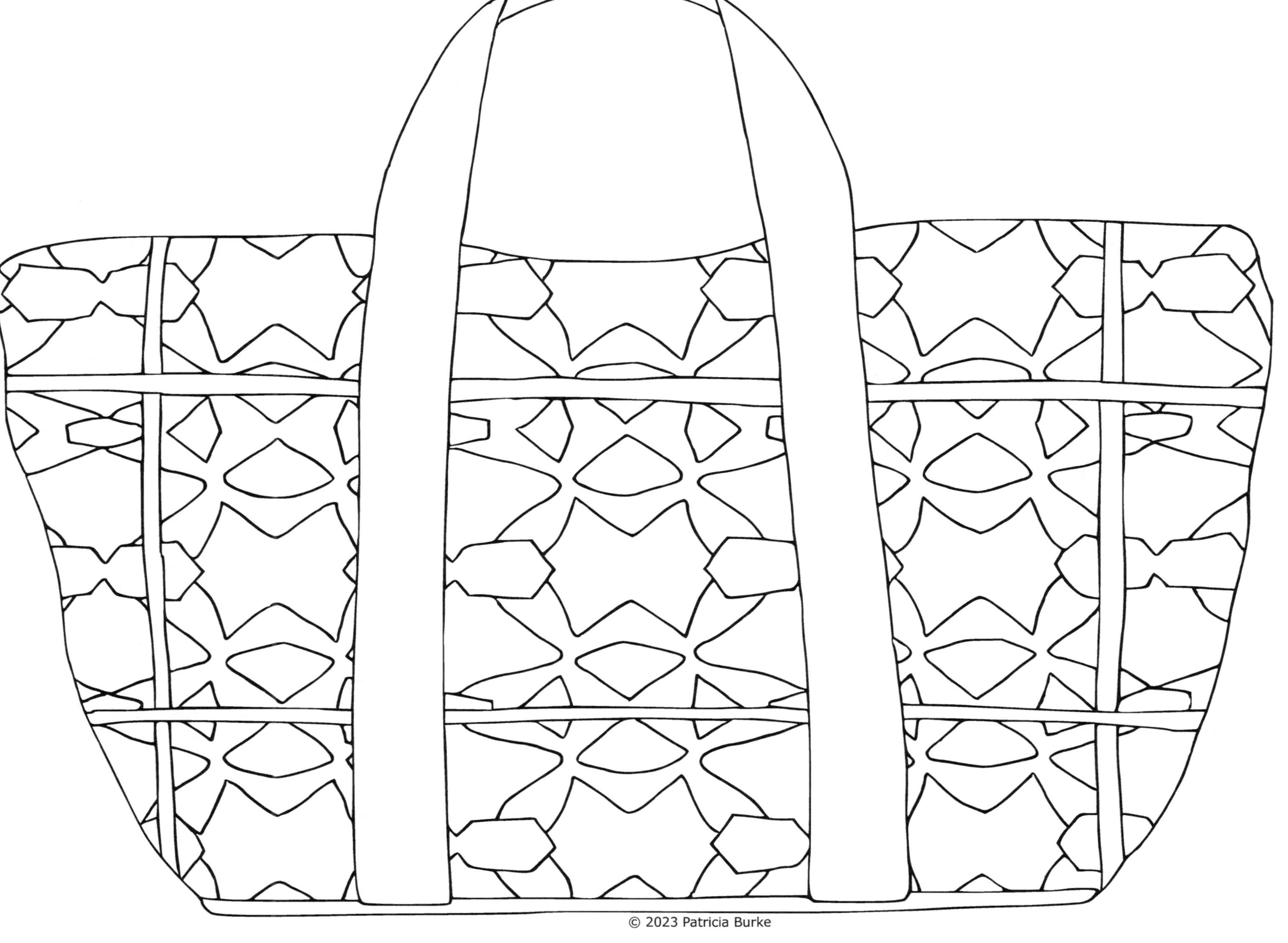

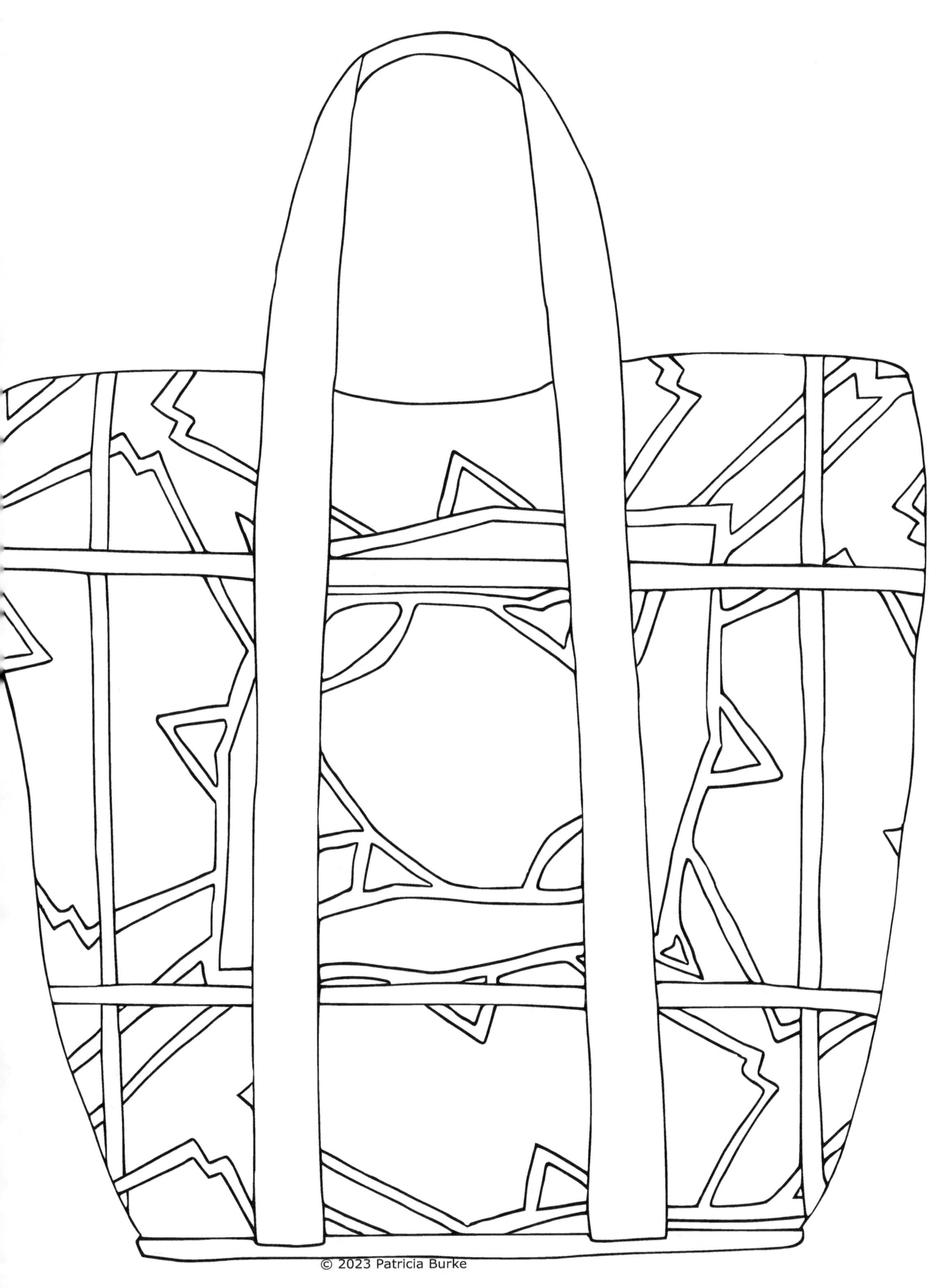

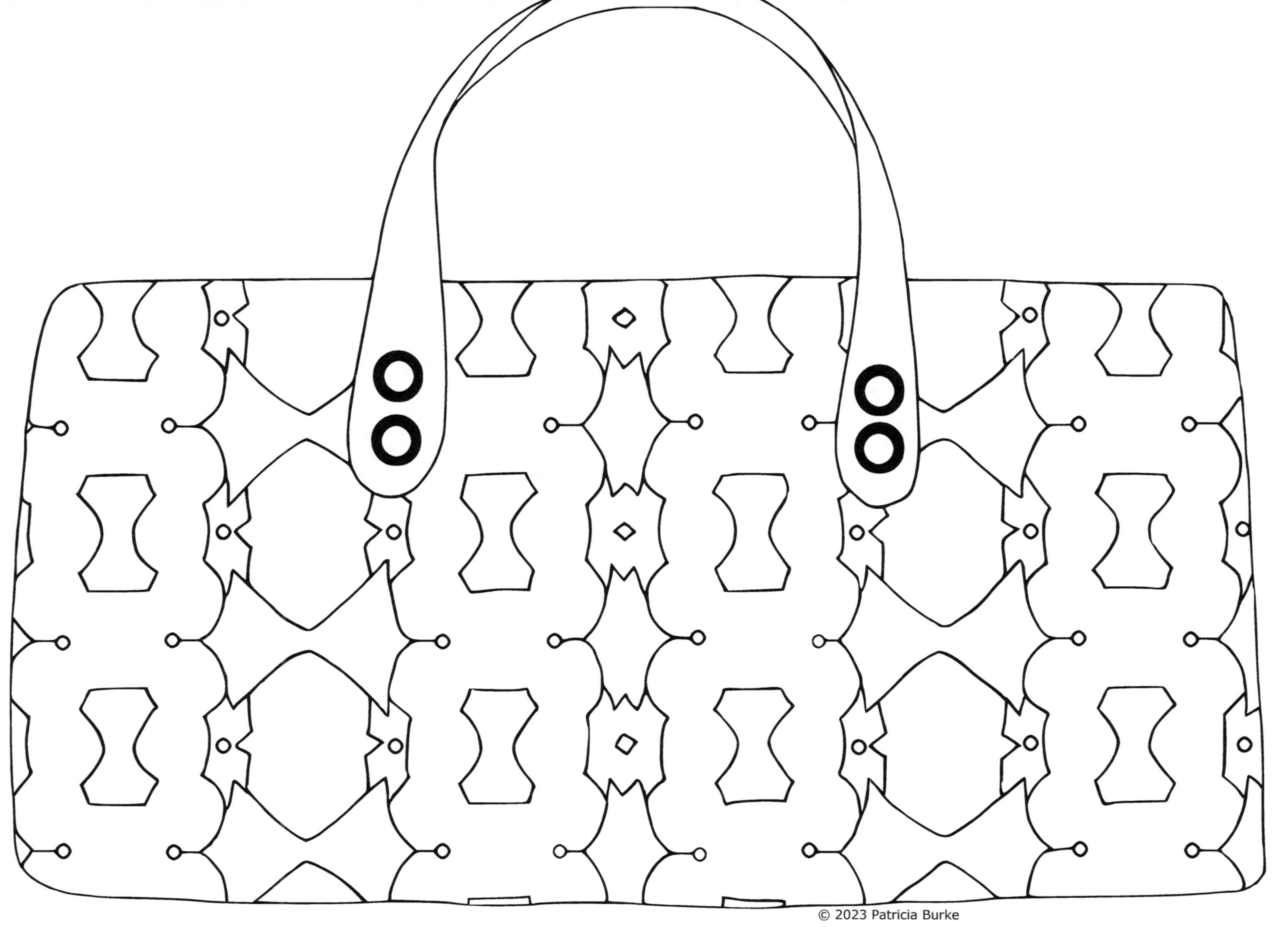

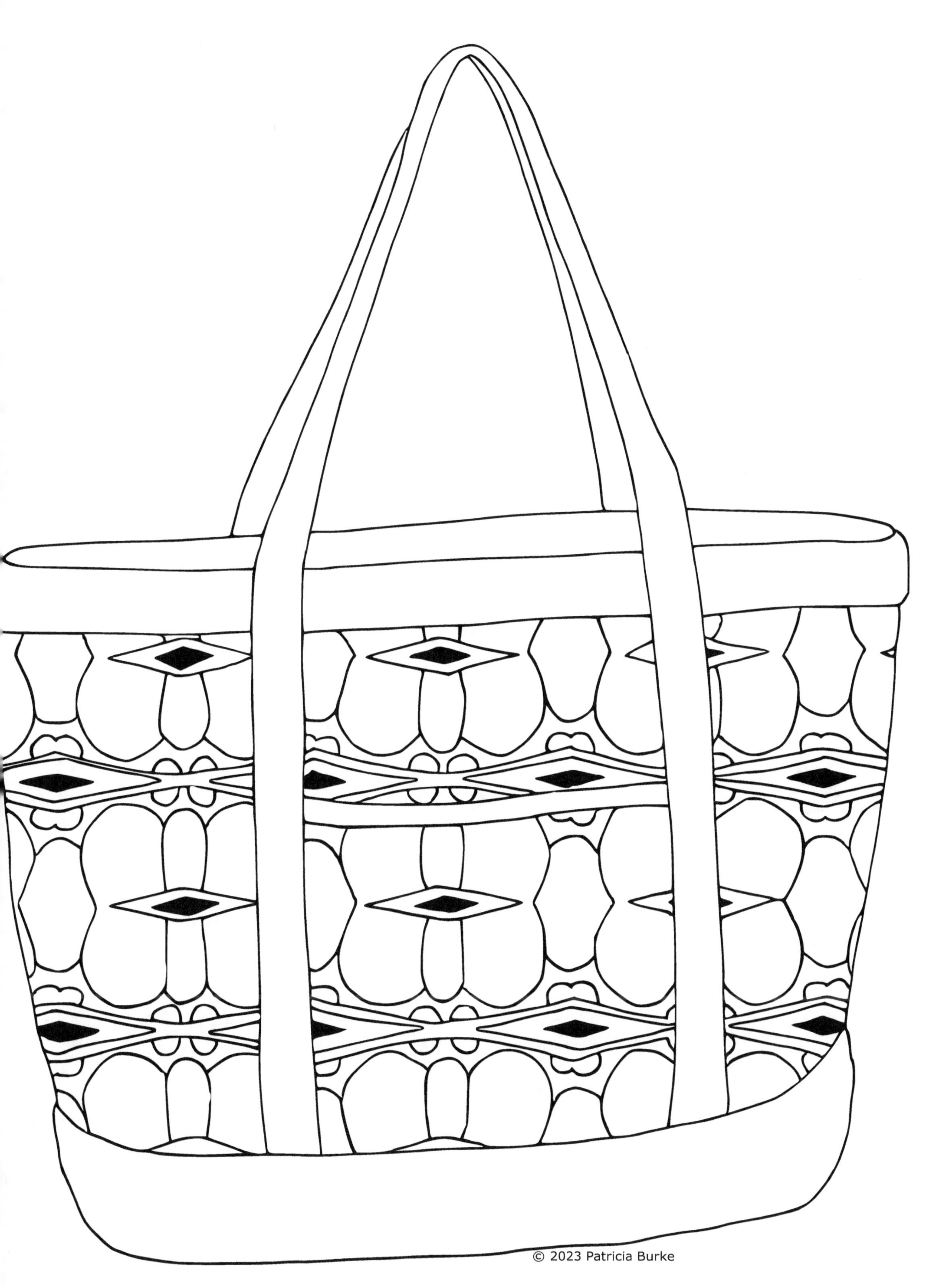

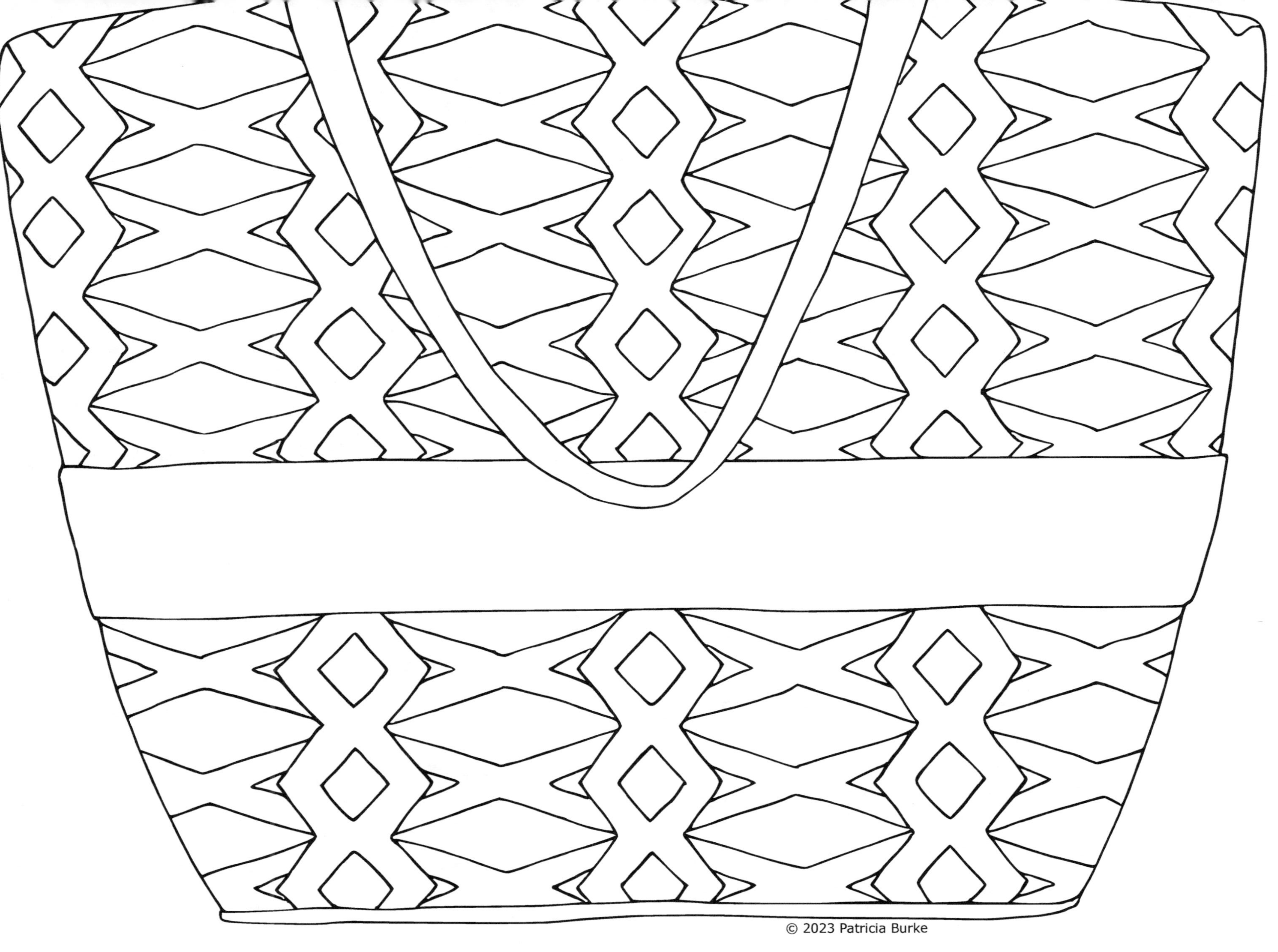

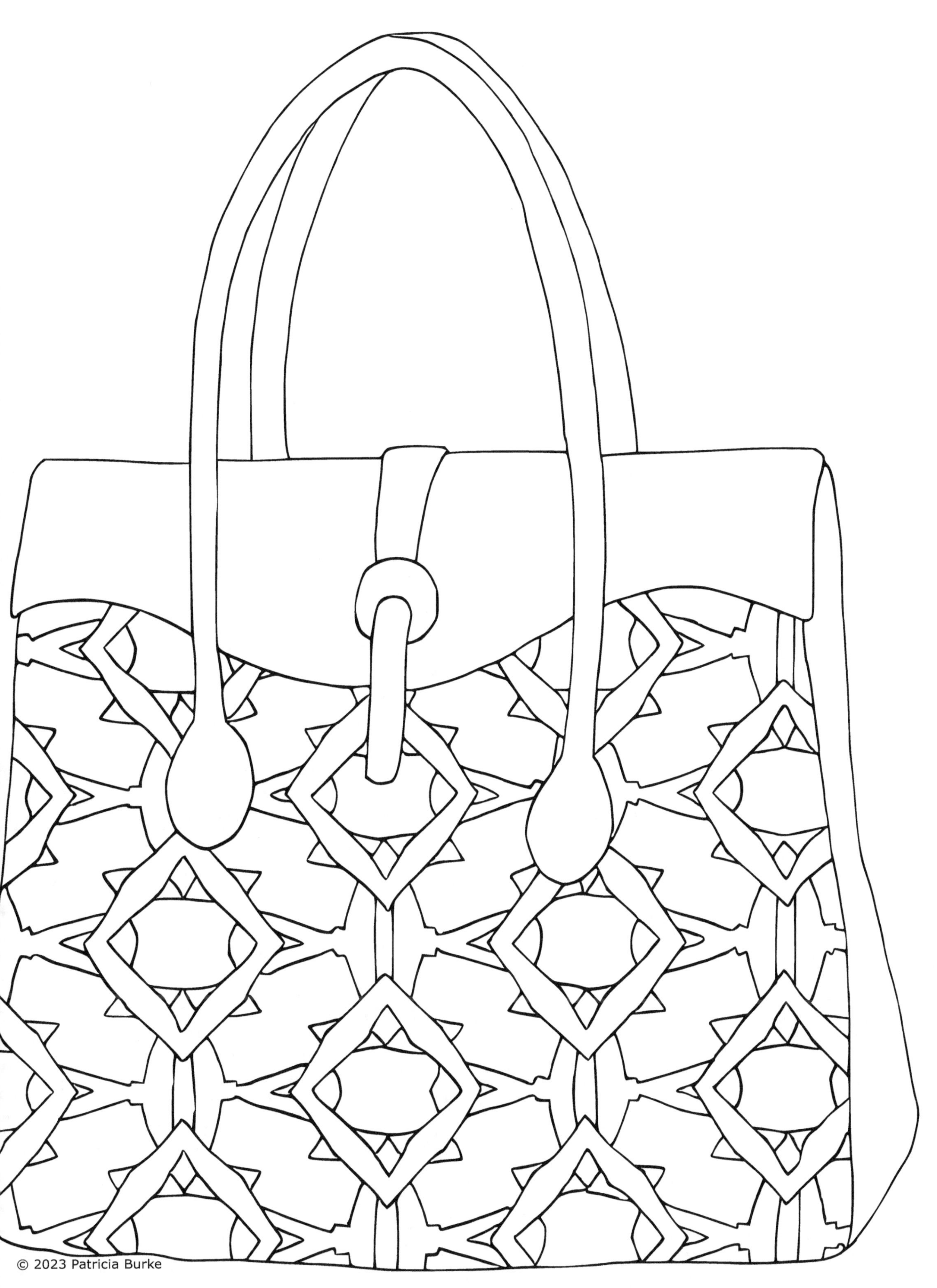

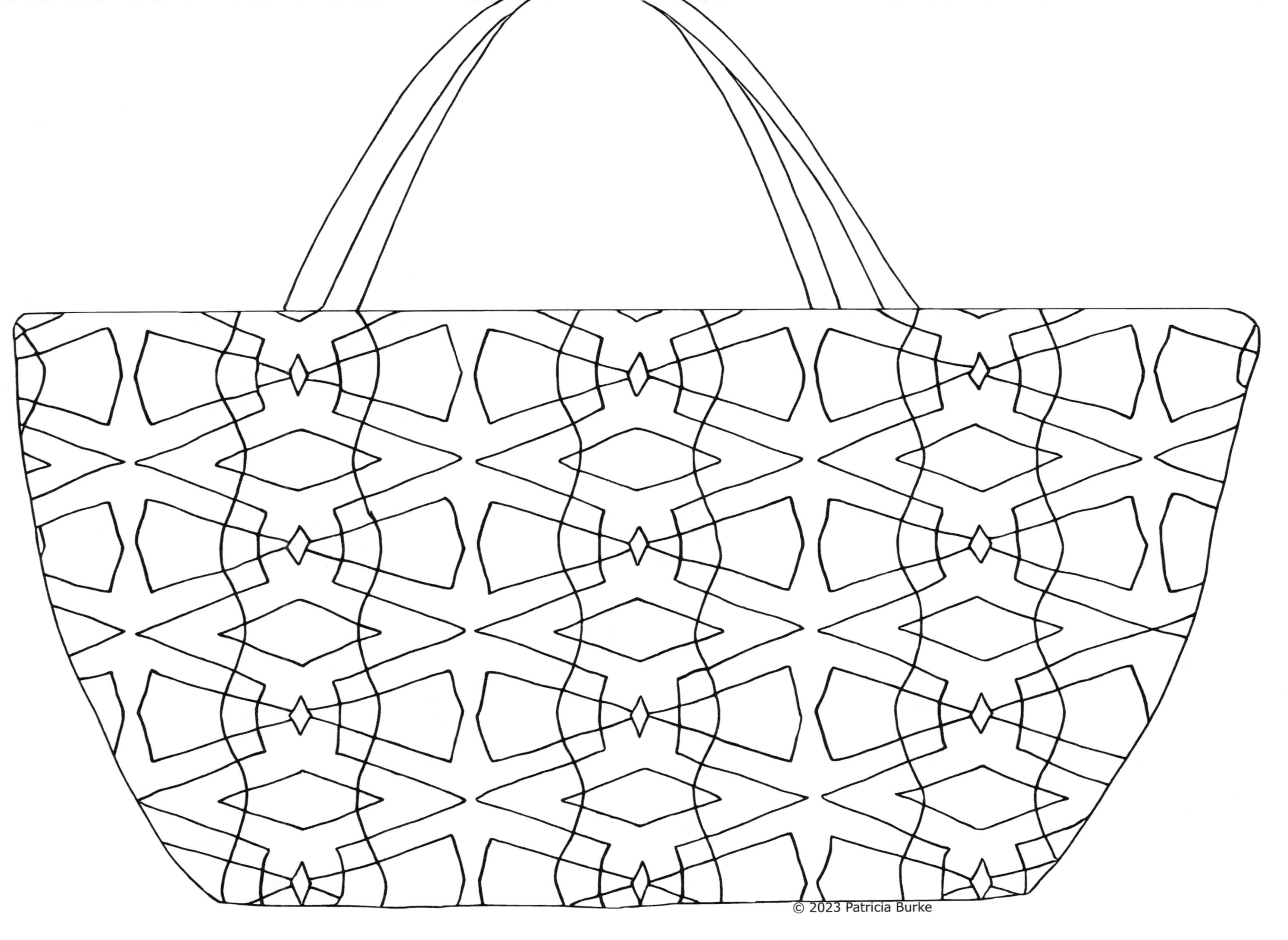

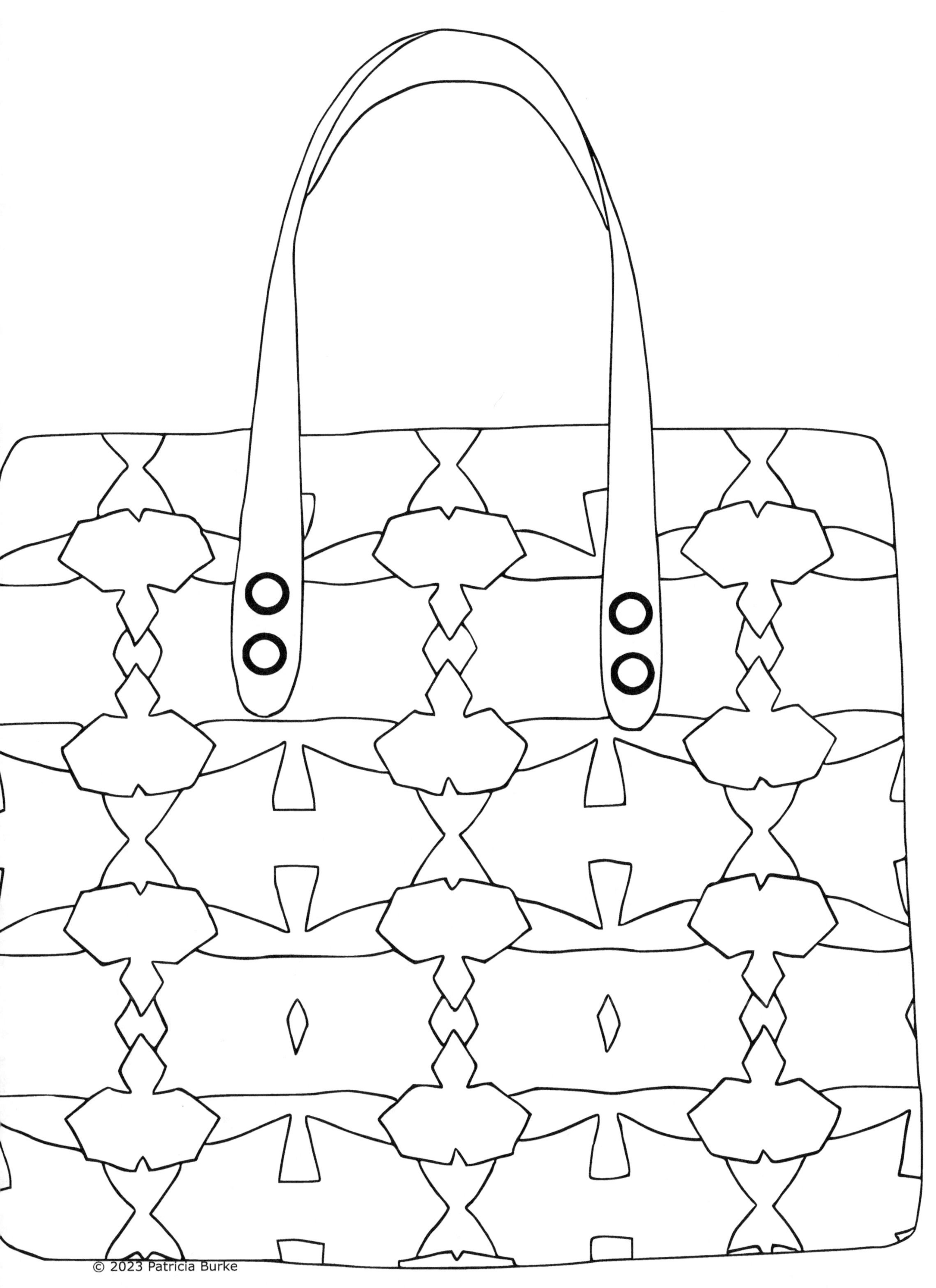

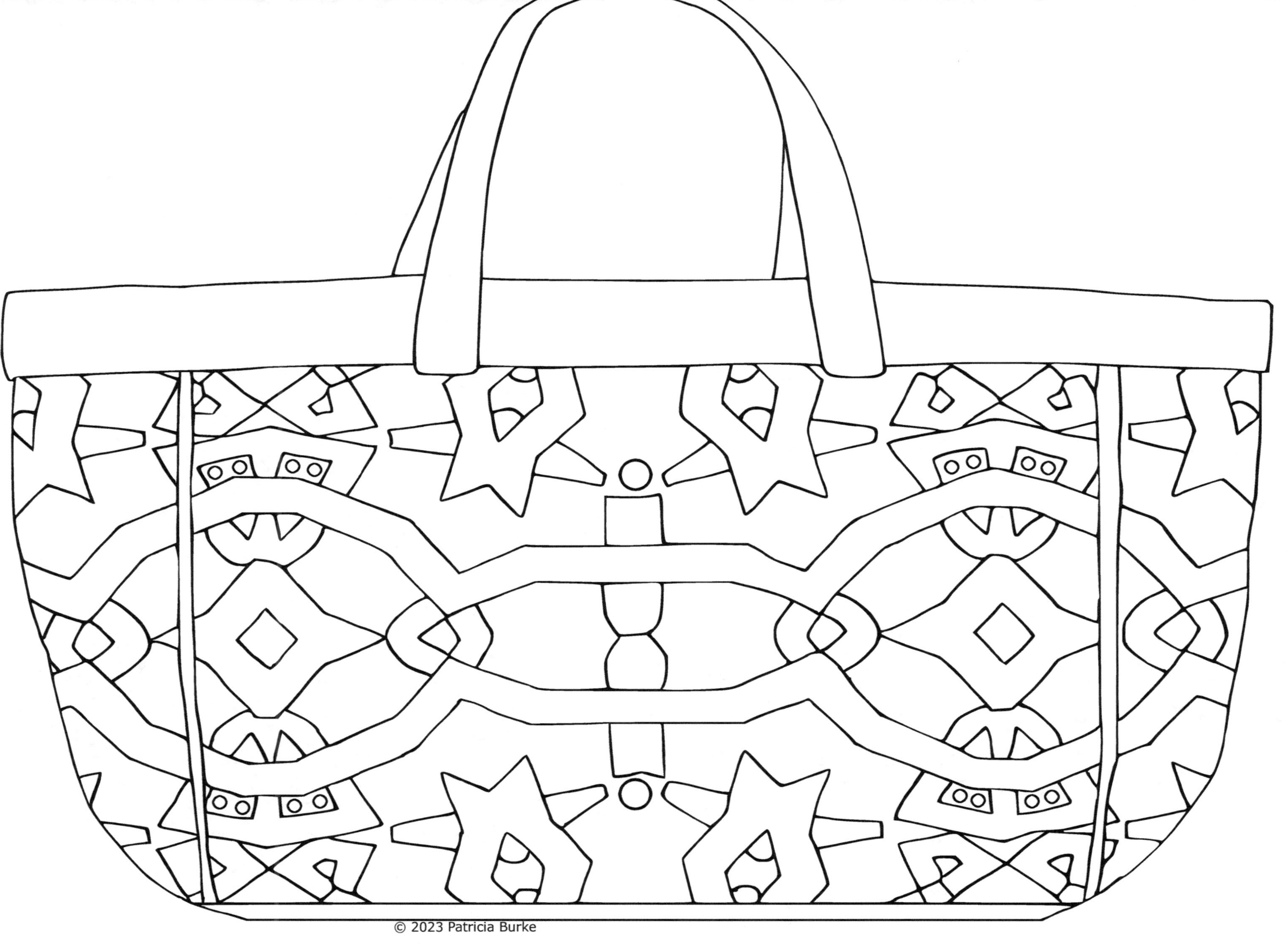

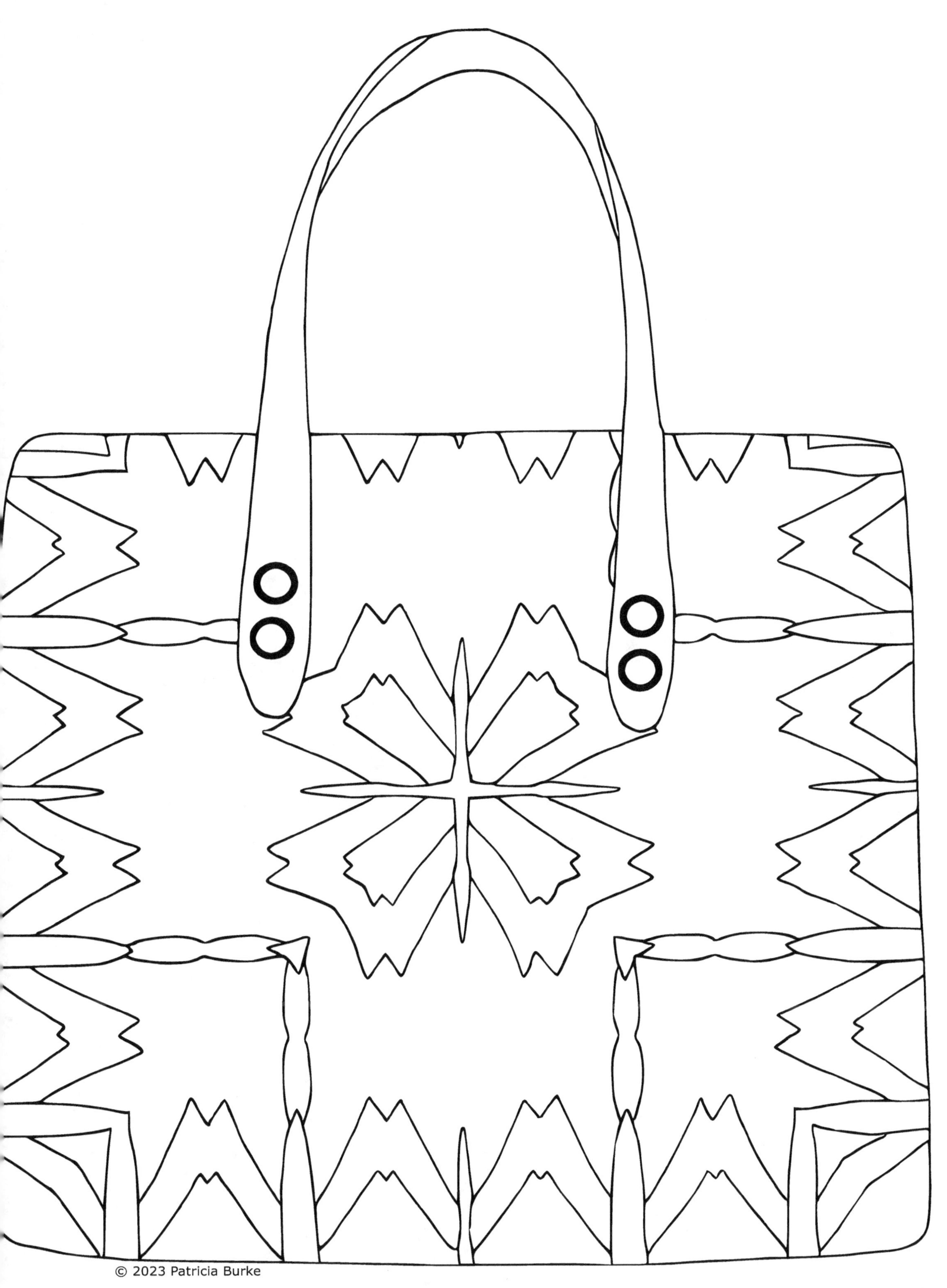

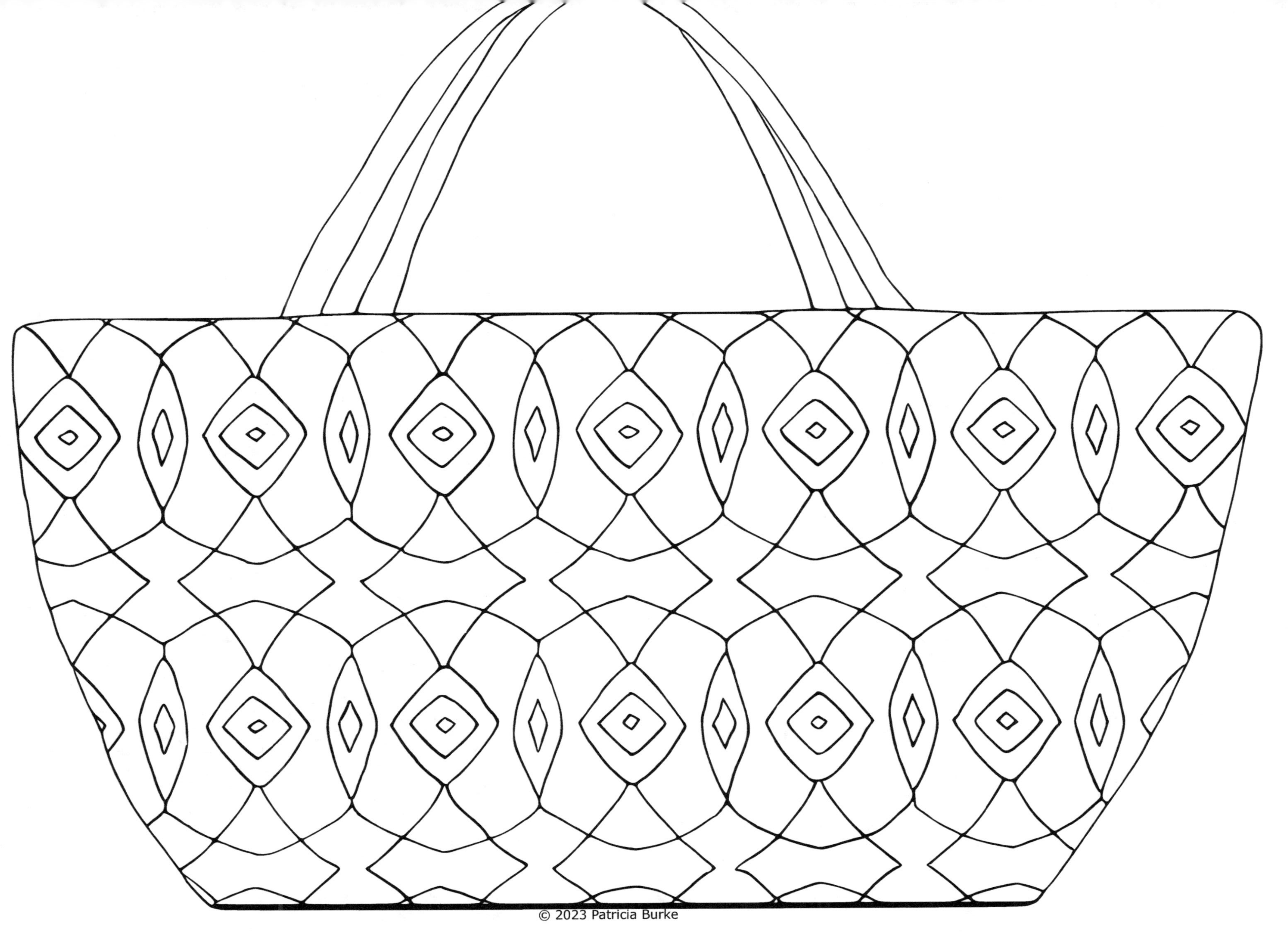

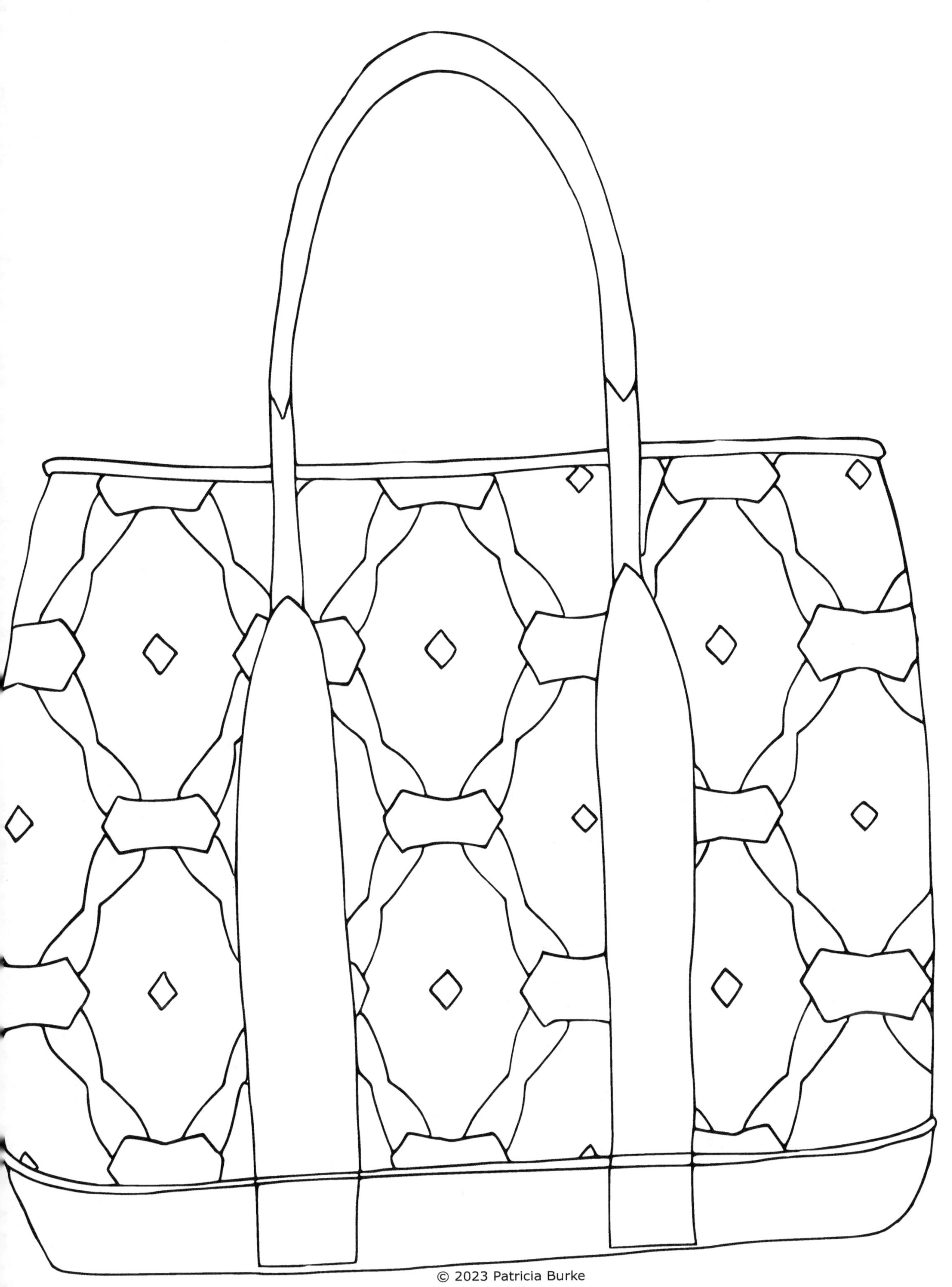

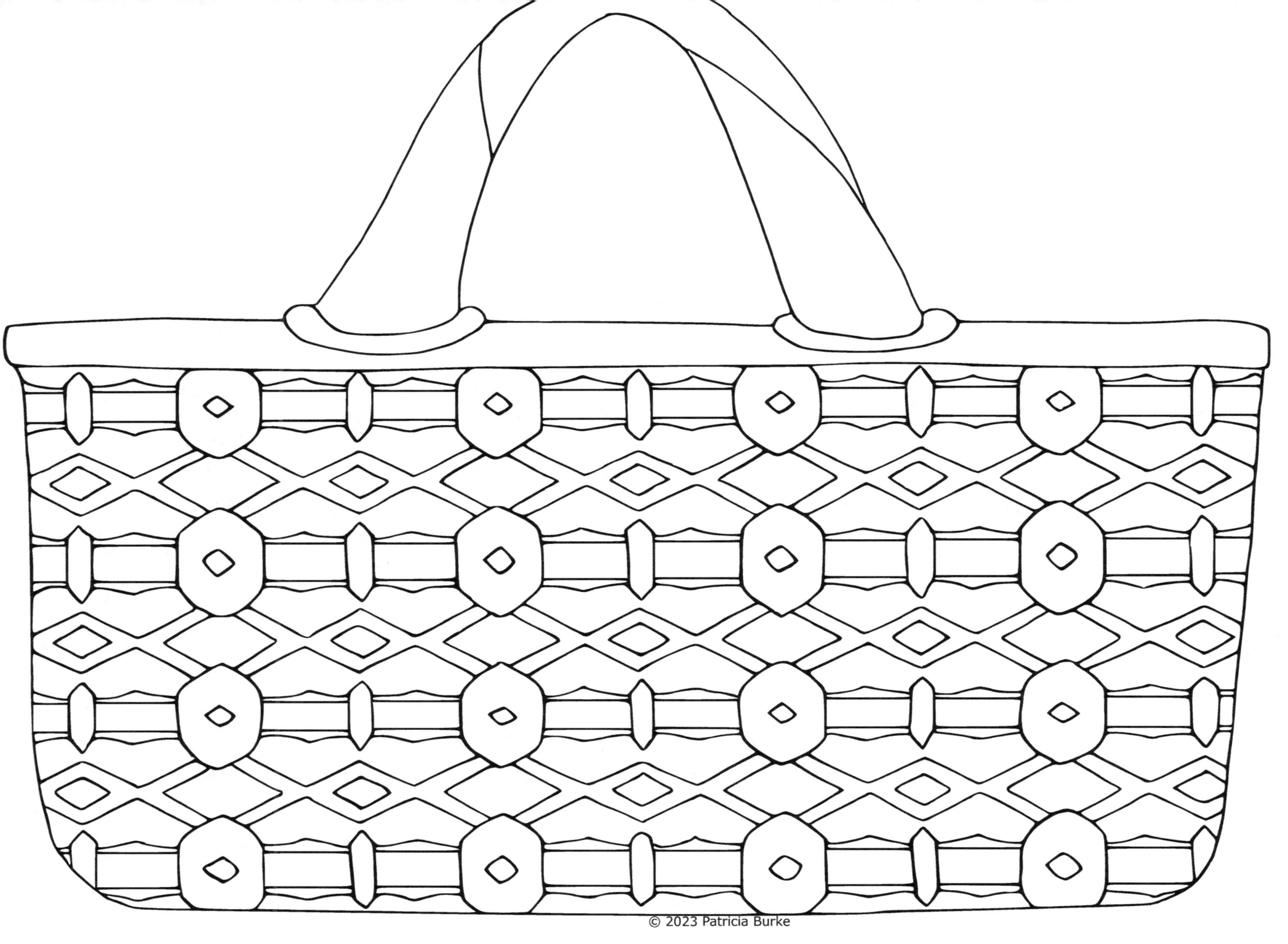

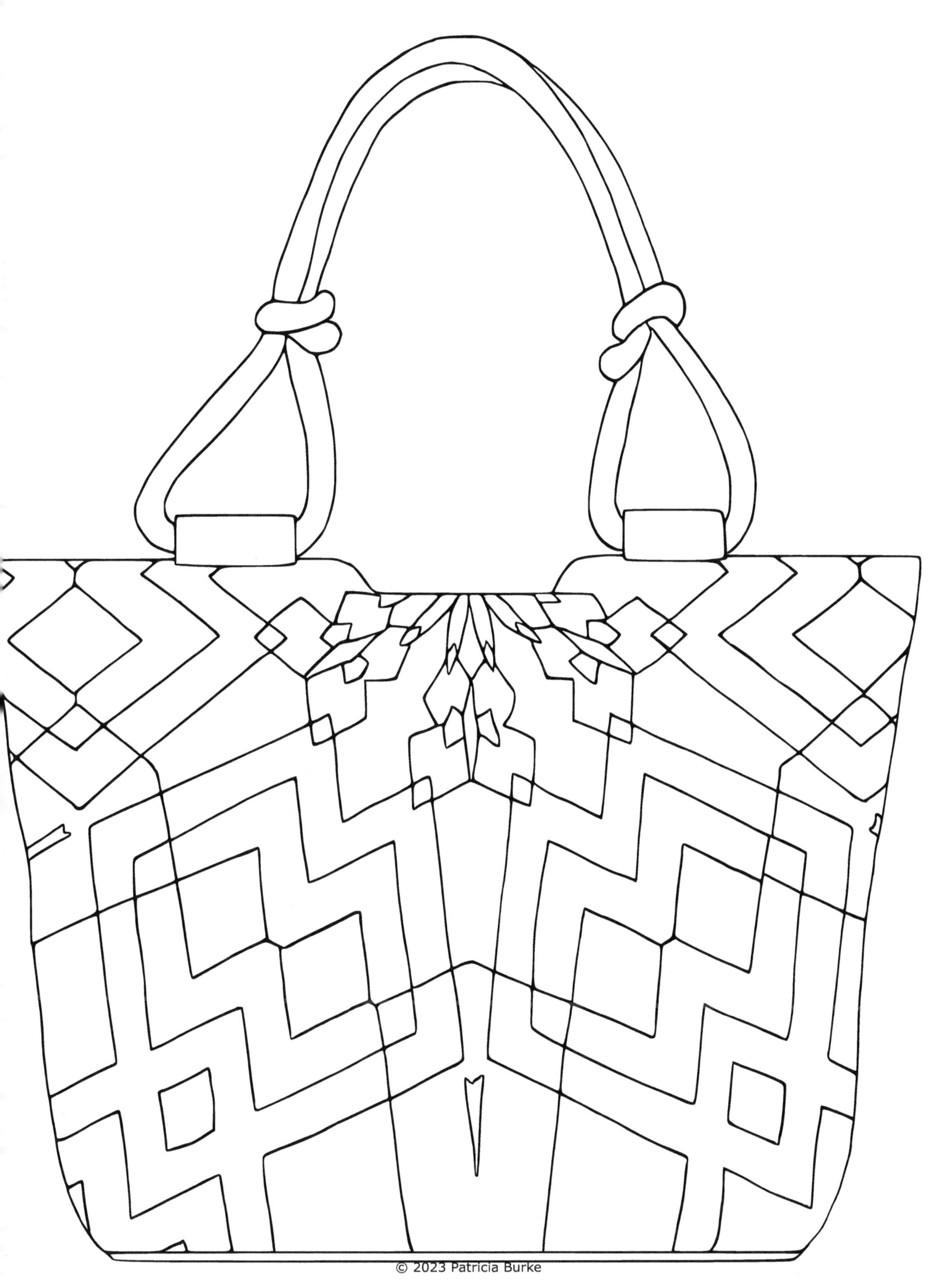

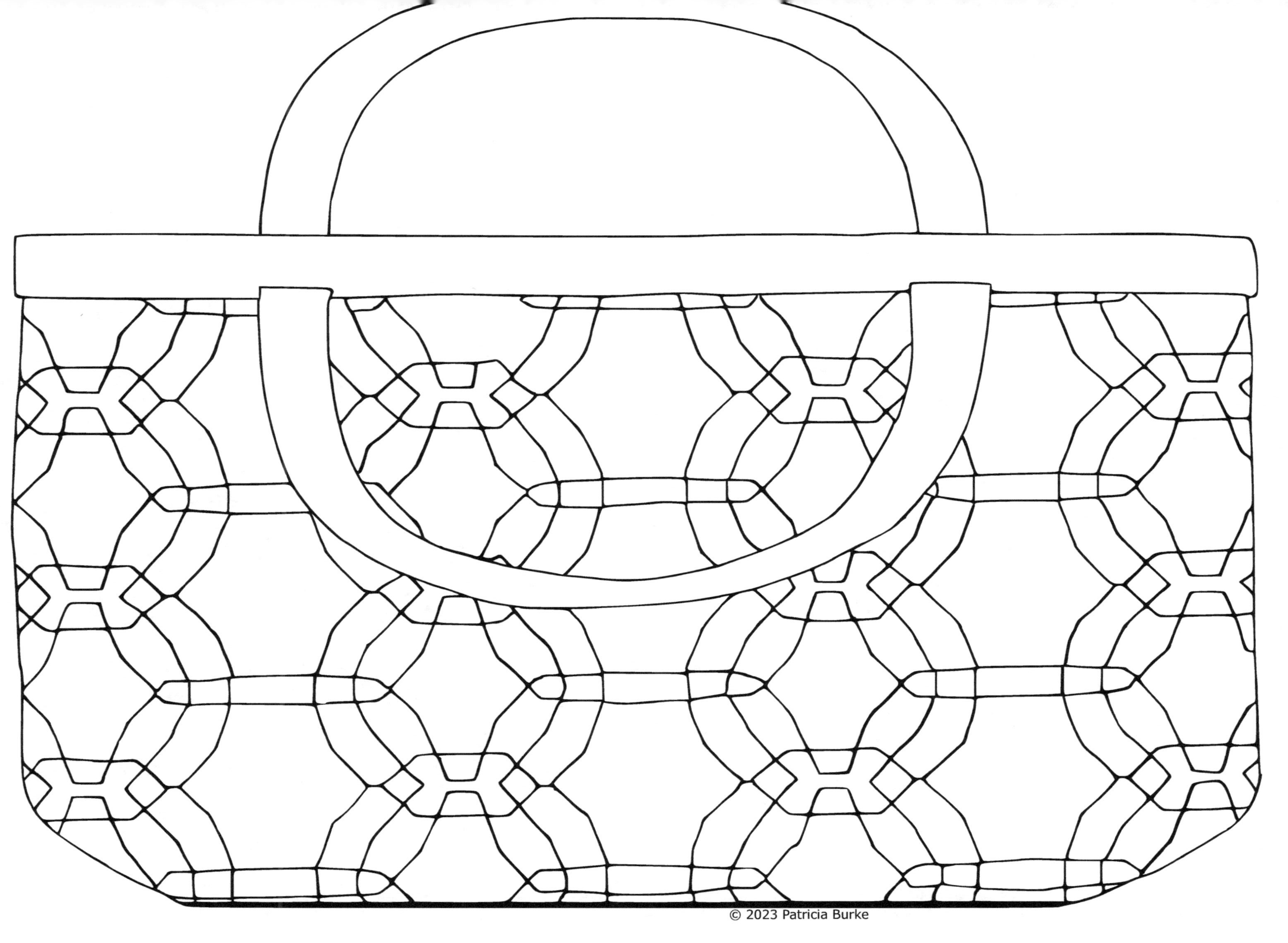

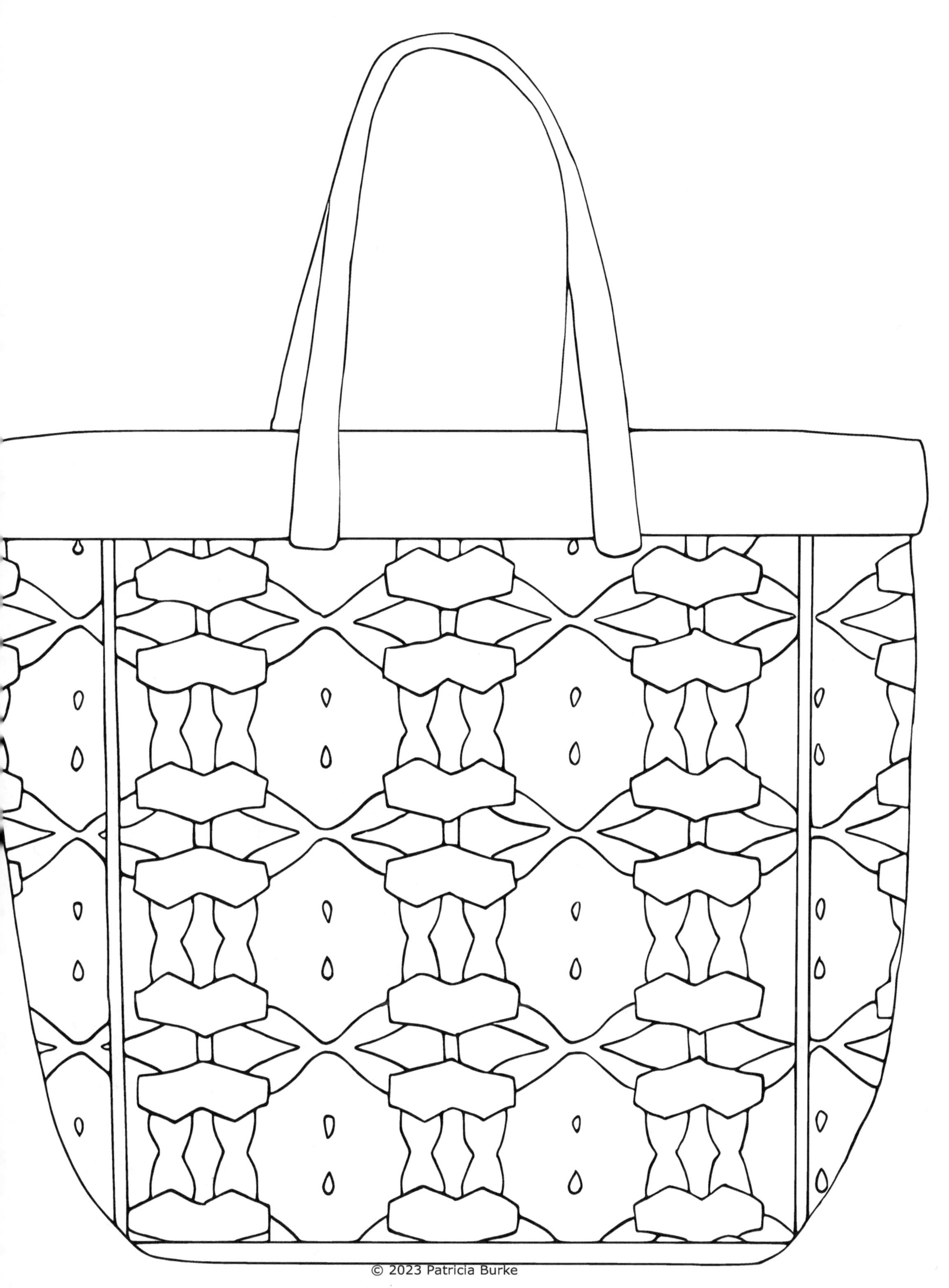

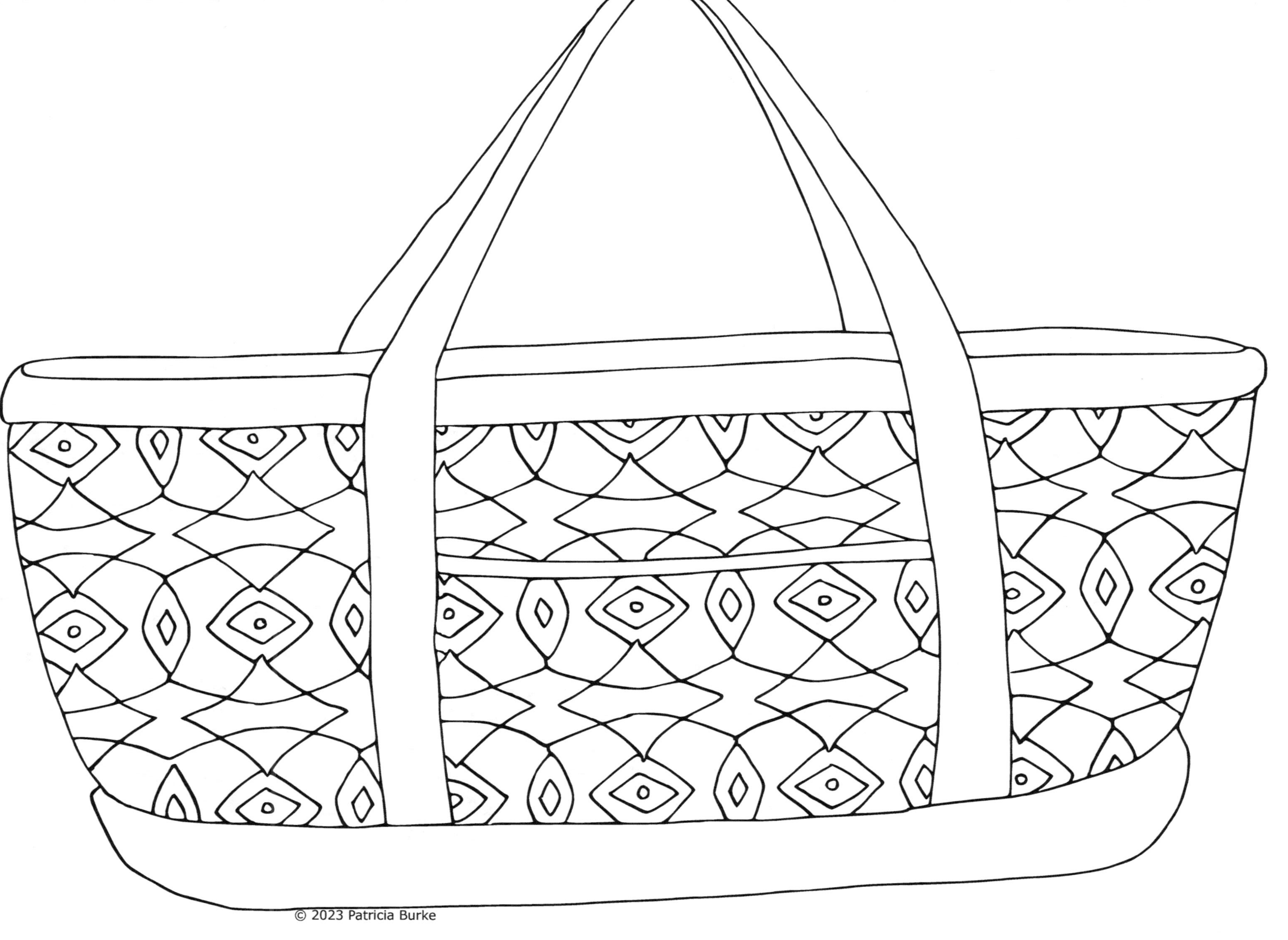

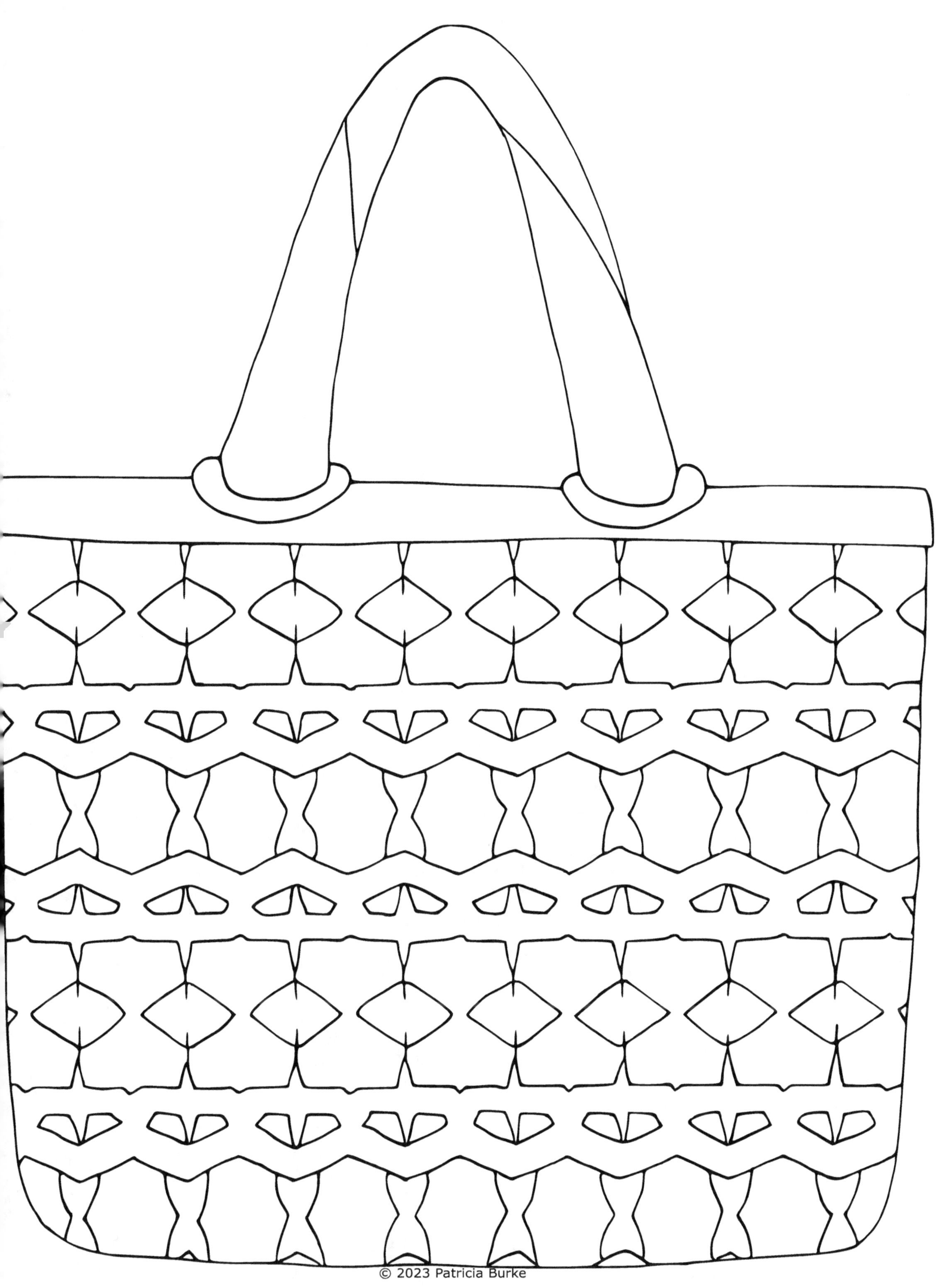

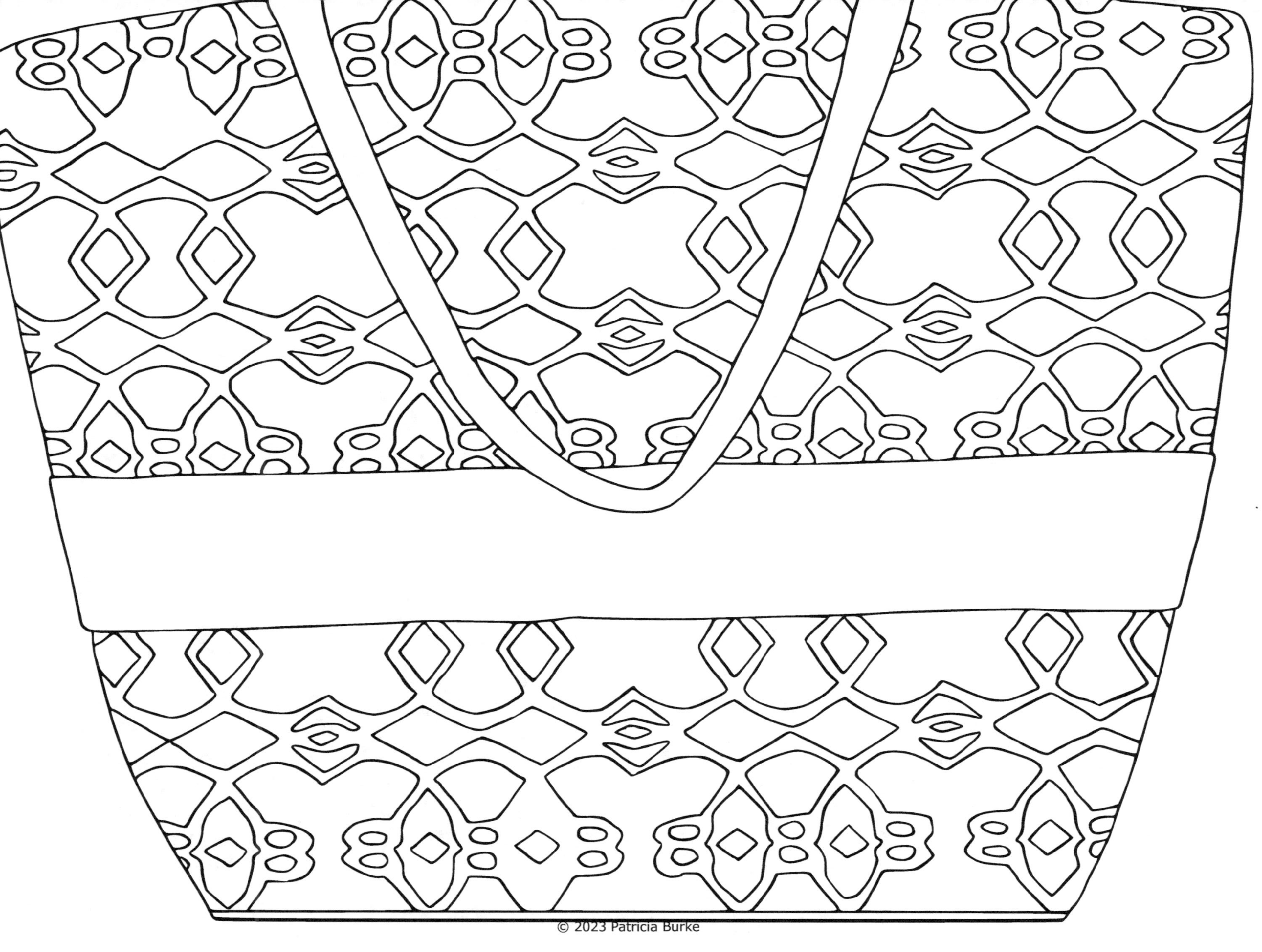

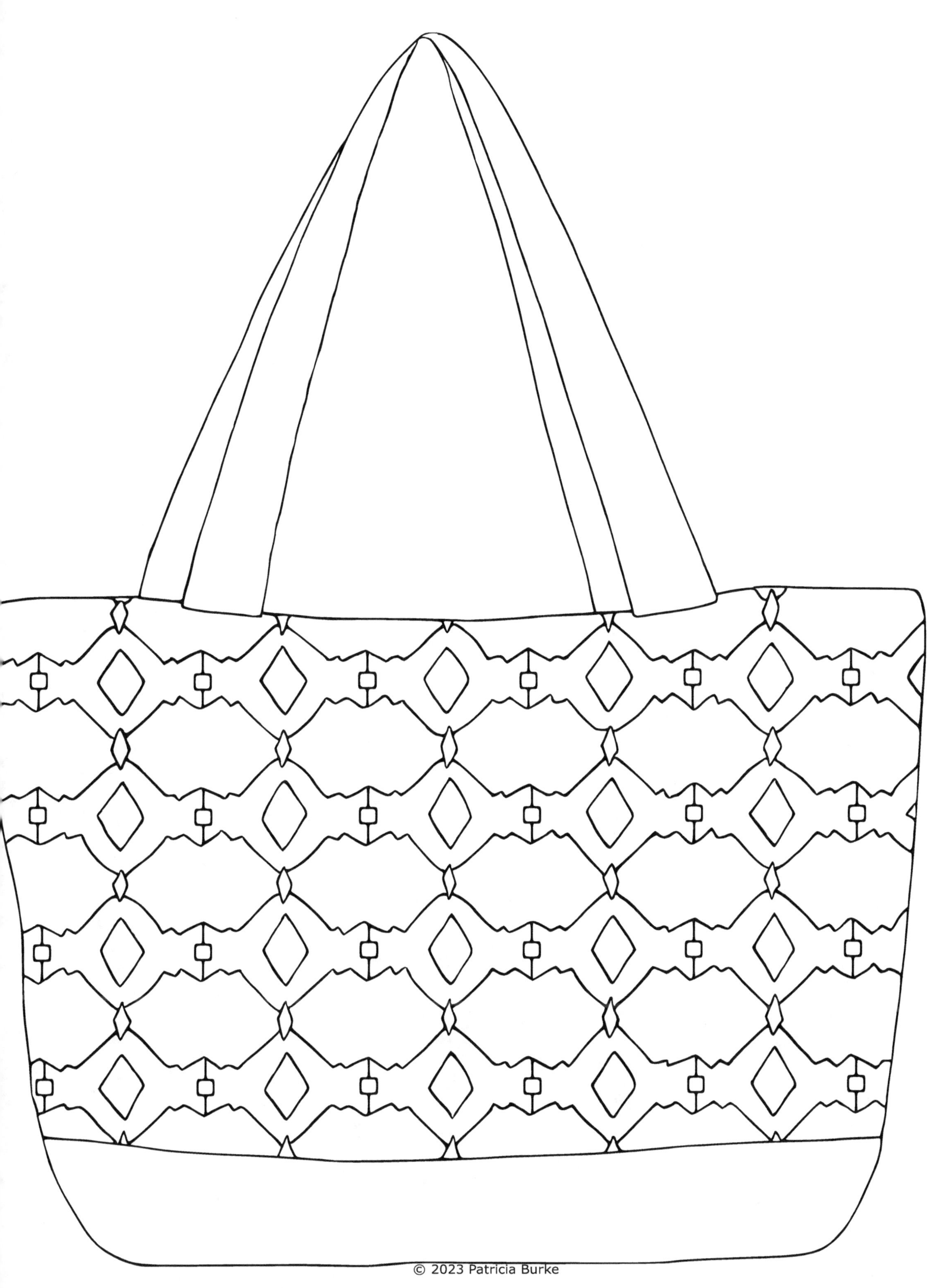

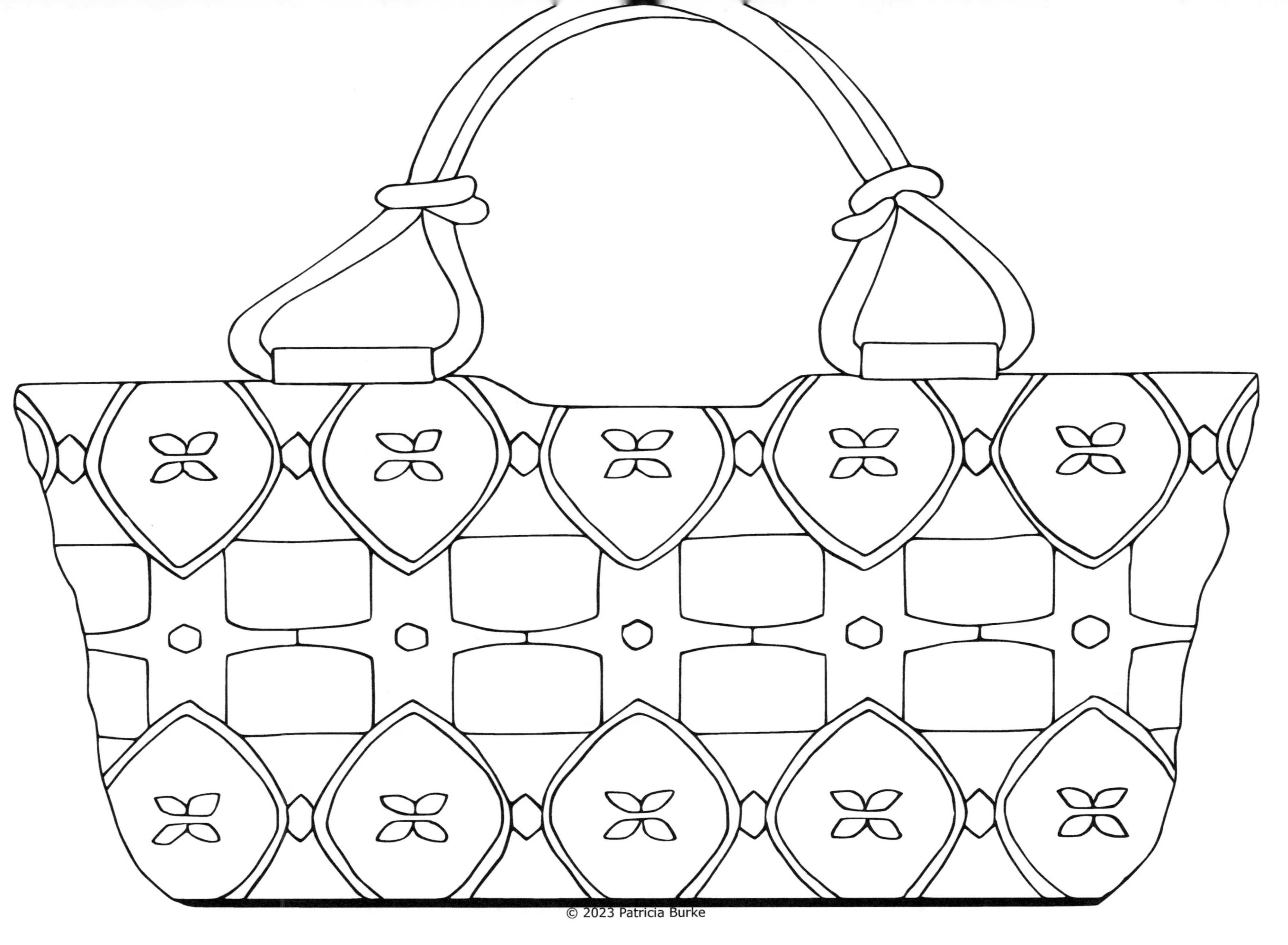

Blotter Page

Blotter Page

Blotter Page

www.ingramcontent.com/pod-product-compliance
Lightning Source LLC
LaVergne TN
LVHW080327110826
845155LV00026B/209

* 9 7 8 1 9 5 1 5 7 6 1 8 9 *